Using the Law
in Social Work

Transforming Social Work Practice – titles in the series

To order, please contact our distributor: BEBC Distribution, Albion Close, Parkstone, Poole, BH12 3LL. Telephone: 0845 230 9000, email: **learningmatters@bebc.co.uk**. You can also find more information on each of these titles and our other learning resources at **www.learningmatters.co.uk**

Using the Law in Social Work

THIRD EDITION

ROBERT JOHNS

Series Editors: Jonathan Parker and Greta Bradley

LearningMatters

First published in 2003 by Learning Matters Ltd.
Reprinted in 2003 and 2004
Second edition 2005
Reprinted in 2006
Third edition 2007
Reprinted in 2008

British Library Cataloguing in Publication Data
A CIP record for this book is available from the British Library.

ISBN: 978 1 84445 114 2

Cover and text design by Code 5 Design Associates Ltd
Project management by Deer Park Productions
Typeset by Pantek Arts Ltd, Maidstone, Kent
Printed and bound in Great Britain by Cromwell Press Ltd, Trowbridge, Wiltshire

Learning Matters Ltd
33 Southernhay East
Exeter EX1 1NX
Tel: 01392 215560
info@learningmatters.co.uk
www.learningmatters.co.uk

Contents

Table of Cases

Table of Legislation

Primary legislation

Secondary legislation

Conventions

'welfare'. The majority of this chapter is taken up with an overview of the legal basis for community care services, but the discussion is also extended to measures by which local authorities, the voluntary sector and independent organisations can protect vulnerable adults who are at risk of various forms of harm.

Chapter 6 is a more specialist chapter, applicable to social workers who work in the field of youth justice. This book does not cover work with adult offenders since in England and Wales this is the prerogative of the National Probation Service. However, social workers are employed in a nationwide network of Youth Offending Teams, multidisciplinary agencies that implement all aspects of youth justice legislation with a prime responsibility for preventing 'offending behaviour'.

Chapter 7 addresses the role of the courts as a key forum in which social workers are held publicly accountable. It focuses on practice issues that sometimes cause social workers anxiety: what actually happens in court, court's expectations, giving evidence in court, writing reports. This chapter highlights the main issues for social workers when they are called to account for their actions. Courts are the forum where the law is put into practice in the sense that cases are 'tried' or 'heard', and where independent decisions are made about social work practice or recommendations. It is therefore essential to understand the role courts play in social work generally, but most especially in the fields of youth justice and child protection.

Finally, Chapter 8 addresses a number of issues that are sometimes overlooked when social workers study the law. For this chapter is not about what social workers do, it is about who they are: their credibility and the standards of professional practice that the public is entitled to expect. The emphasis in this chapter is on public accountability in the sense of ensuring that high standards of professional practice are maintained. What legal provisions exist to ensure that social workers are reliable and trustworthy? What standards apply to the kinds of services provided, especially in relation to residential care? How are social workers accountable to service users and employers?

The book concludes with an overview of its coverage, indicating areas for further study and urging a watching brief on the ever-changing world of social work law.

Each chapter begins with a reference to the relevant occupational standards together with a summary of the chapter contents. The structure of each chapter varies, but in all cases there will be illustrative case material incorporated into the discussion. In keeping the discussion practical yet clarifying a number of complex issues, it is necessary to make some accommodation for readers' and social work practitioners' needs and so the following points need to be borne in mind.

- This book should not be treated as an authoritative statement of the law – it is intended as an introduction to relevant law, not an advanced legal textbook.

- Legislative sources will be cited as accurately as possible, but extensive quotation of legislation is avoided, so if you need to refer to specific sections of particular Acts you will need to use additional sources such as other textbooks and the internet (see Further Reading and website addresses at the end of each chapter).

- Professional practice and decision-making should not be based solely on this book, which is intended as an introductory text for professional qualifying courses in social work (BA or MA in Social Work).

- This text does not cover every aspect of social work law, but should provide some indication of the areas which are of most direct relevance to practice in England and Wales.

- There are major differences in the law in Scotland and Northern Ireland, and significant differences in relation to Wales. Whilst every effort has been made to incorporate legislation and guidance in relation to Wales, practitioners may need to double check on references to regulations and current policy.

Whilst the book is as accurate as possible at the time of going to press, legislation and practice is constantly changing, so it is important to check out the latest legislation.

Chapter outline

This chapter sets the scene by setting out a number of reasons as to why the law is an integral part of good social work practice. It is important to be clear about why the law is relevant, and how a detailed knowledge of what the law actually says is sometimes necessary for social work practitioners – this book sets out precisely those areas where social workers need to be thoroughly familiar with the law in everyday practice. The law is a major way in which people's rights are promoted, offering protection from discrimination, informing social workers and social work agencies of what they can and cannot do, and at a broader level clarifying the relationship between the state and the individual or family. Social workers need to know about all of this. The majority of this chapter therefore is given over to a consideration of how the law sets the boundaries for social work practice. It does this through a 'case study' – not the usual kind of case study where we look at the needs of a family or individual, but a policy case study, an example of how the law has developed in relation to one area of social work practice. The case study in question is the events that occurred in Cleveland in the mid-1980s that led to a highly influential government report that became a blueprint for the relationship between the state, social work and the family. Do remember though when you read this case study that it is simply meant as an example of how changes in the law occur. It is the 'peg' on which to hang explanations of how the law changes and why. It is hoped that you will find this more interesting than simply reading a dry account of political and legal processes. By proceeding through this case example, you will encounter a number of terms which may be new to you; it may be helpful for you to note these as you proceed, so that you build up your own glossary of legal terms.

Why law?

In order to explain the importance of law to social work practice, it is necessary to reflect on the roles and responsibilities of social workers and how they might impinge on people's everyday lives.

The majority of social workers in Britain today are employed by publicly accountable organisations – local authorities or agencies directly commissioned by them. Much of social workers' professional lives are spent in providing services to people and, in some cases, intervening in people's lives in order to protect them from themselves or other people.

Immediately it becomes obvious that social workers are deeply involved in issues to do with people's rights: rights of access to information, rights and entitlements to services, rights to be protected from harm. The extent to which social workers can offer services and can offer protection is bound to be determined by some kind of framework, and that framework is, of course, the law. So it is essential for social workers to know about the law.

ACTIVITY *1.1*

Why else might social workers need to know about the law?
List as many reasons as you can for social workers learning about the law.

There are a number of reasons you could have listed so don't worry if what you have does not quite correspond to what follows. Generally, social workers need to know about the law because:

- it tells them what their powers and duties are;

- in some areas of practice it sets out what they have to do, what they have discretion to do, and what they may not do;

- it sets out clear lines of accountability which can include bodies that adjudicate when necessary;

- it ensures that processes whereby decisions are made are fair and equitable;

- it may help clarify ethical practice issues;

- through the court system, the law makes or ratifies decisions made by social work agencies;

- it acts as a final arbiter between social workers and service users where there is a dispute that cannot be resolved by any other means.

It may be also worth mentioning some things that the law cannot do. The law cannot tell social workers what to do in every circumstance: it can only set out a framework. The law cannot resolve the everyday tensions and dilemmas of social work practice, since there is no ready prescription for resolving the complex problems that sometimes confront social workers. Above all, the law cannot substitute for sound professional practice. Critically, social workers need to abide by a code of ethics and set of practice principles that are over and beyond what the law may offer. In this respect it is important to acknowledge that there may occasionally be a conflict between the law and social work values. For example, social work has a strong commitment to anti-oppressive practice. When it comes to counteracting discrimination in relation to race, the law supports and indeed encourages the anti-discriminatory approach of much social work practice (in particular the Race Relations Amendment Act 2000 directs local authorities to promote anti-racist policies). Yet until its repeal by the Local Government Act 2003, section 28 Local Government Act 1988 prohibited the promotion of homosexuality by local authorities, a law that clearly conflicted with social work values and principles which require people of different sexual orientations to be treated equitably. Furthermore, there is a danger that in seeing the law as the ultimate determinant of social work practice the practitioner might then look to the law for 'easy' solutions to complex problems. For example, it is sometimes not easy to decide how exactly a child's cultural needs are to be met when it is necessary to provide a foster care placement outside of that child's own family. It would be easy if the law said that children can only be offered placements with foster carers whose background matched the child's, yet the law does not say this. Instead it declares the general principle that local authorities should take this factor into account when placing a child. Likewise, it is tempting to expect the law to determine when some child-rearing practices are abusive, yet the law cannot do this because so much depends on the context and the intention of those who are parenting the child. When you are more experienced as a practitioner, you will undoubtedly have to return to these sorts of dilemmas and may sometimes find the law frustrating where it does not apparently offer clear direction or guidance.

The whole issue of the extent to which the law should be involved in everyday social work decisions was a key issue that arose in the Cleveland case. This case has been chosen precisely because it says a great deal about the role of the law and social work, and also sets out the framework for the relationship between the state (the government) and families who can justifiably claim rights to determine their own lives, rights that are now enshrined in Article 8 European Convention on Human Rights (1950) (see discussion in Chapter 2).

What went wrong in Cleveland?

The integration of social services through the amalgamation of former children's departments, welfare departments and certain health-related functions was brought about by the implementation of the Seebohm Report (1968) which was translated into law through the Local Authority Social Services Act 1970. A number of issues quickly emerged in relation to the protection of children that resulted in what appeared to be an unending series of inquiries that started with the Colwell Inquiry in 1974 (DHSS, 1974), although this was not the first example of inquiries into child abuse (Packman, 1975, Chapter 8). These inquiries focused on the apparent lack of competence and professionalism in social workers who had 'failed' to protect children from death at the hands of a parent or carer, although there was also a feeling that social work itself was being undermined for political reasons (Parton, 1985). The findings of these inquiries were bought together by the Department of Health (1991a) who drew lessons from them which, together with the research-based findings (Aldgate, 2001), are important reading for intending practitioners in this field. In the majority of these cases social workers were criticised for their lack of action, whereas in Cleveland the issue was over-readiness, indeed alleged zealous enthusiasm, for intervening in families in order to 'protect' children. The Cleveland Inquiry was instigated as a result of a large number of children being taken into care against the wishes of parents on the grounds that they were possibly sexually abused. The social services department and the local consultant paediatrician worked together in identifying what they thought were cases of serious abuse, but at that time the law afforded only limited provision for oversight of decisions to take children away from their parents by force. Furthermore, it appeared to be extraordinarily difficult for parents to challenge the diagnosis of the paediatrician and the professional practice of social workers. The following extracts from the Cleveland Report provide a flavour of the kind of issues confronting parents and children.

CASE STUDY

2.12 A number of parents complained that their consent was not sought or not obtained for medical examinations; or for the taking of photographs; or for disclosure work to be carried out with their children.

2.17 Grandparents, who were bringing up their 10-year-old grandson, told the Inquiry: We were simply told by a social worker [named] that [our grandson] had to be examined and our permission was not sought.

2.25 … received a letter from social worker which referred to children she (Mother) might have in the future and which included: '… there would be no guarantees from us that you would be entrusted to look after any children you may have.' The mother said she was pregnant at this time but as a consequence of receiving this letter the pregnancy was terminated.

2.34 The parents of three children aged 9, 7 and just under 2 years, described the total denial of access to their children both whilst in hospital and in foster care …

2.36 Many parents felt strongly that they should be heard at case conferences. A number told the Inquiry that they were informed that case conferences were to be held. Some said they were told they could not attend. Others said they were informed they could attend but would not be admitted or would not be heard whilst the meeting was in progress. Some said they were told the results of case conferences. Others complained they were told neither of case conferences nor of decisions reached there.

2.52 …The parents' complaints were threefold:

1. They were denied or unable to obtain information about their children or what was happening or what was planned for the future;

2. That social workers were not interested in and not enquiring into the family environment and history; and

3. That paediatricians and social workers had concluded that the parent (usually father) or parents were abusers and, until that was accepted by one or both, were indifferent, unresponsive and lacked compassion.

2.53 The father of one family referred to making numerous calls to social services but to being met with what can only be described as utter stonewalling.

(extracts from DHSS, 1988, pp38–44)

These are simply a few extracts that give a flavour of the issues at stake. It is easy to see straight away how parents saw themselves as being totally undermined and abused by professional action and the lack of legal safeguards. Critically, they were not afforded proper rights to present their views, a complaint echoed by service users in other areas of social work practice (Clarke, 1993, Chapter 5). Yet the Cleveland Report goes much further than this and acknowledges the underlying dilemma of child protection work, namely that social workers are *damned if they do, and damned if they don't* – pilloried if they fail to act when they should have done (with the benefit of hindsight), and castigated if they seemed to be too ready to remove children. The specific legal issues were:

- the law as it then existed appeared to offer few avenues for parents to challenge social workers' or paediatricians' decisions;

- magistrates appeared to rubber stamp decisions and did not really call social workers or doctors to account for their actions;

- there appeared to be limited avenues of redress, with few appeal possibilities;

- children could be kept in care for some considerable time without anyone having to justify to the courts substantive reasons why they should be;

- the courts and the legal system generally appeared to be weighted against parents, in an adversarial system where the child's voice could not be heard;

- children were seen as objects of concern and not the central subjects of the court proceedings.

There were a whole host of other professional practice issues, not least of which was the relationship between different professions, including the police, but our concern here is to focus on the issue of rights and what this case demonstrates about the operation of the legal system.

It is apparent from the above that the legal system pre-Cleveland offered few safeguards for parents or children, and there was lack of clarity about the role of the law and more specifically the courts. The public furore aroused by Cleveland led to Parliamentary debates and a clear commitment to change the law. The Butler-Sloss Inquiry (DHSS, 1988) promoted the idea that the law needed to be much clearer in establishing the boundaries between parents, children and social workers. In addition, the law needed to take a much more active role in regulating social work practice – not with a view to constraining it, but in order to clarify where and when social workers should intervene on children's behalf. The report also very strongly promoted the idea that the child should be the primary focus of the law's concern, and this particular area of the law needed far greater attention generally.

As a consequence Parliament passed the Children Act 1989. This legislation addressed many of the issues highlighted by the Cleveland incident and in particular clarified the ways in which the law was to protect children. Chapter 4 will explain what the law says and how it relates to current social work practice, but in this chapter we need to explore the background to the Act. Why was the law changed? How does a law get changed? What kind of law is the Children Act 1989 and what other kinds of laws are there? How does legislation such as the Children Act 1989 operate so as to set boundaries but without interfering too much in everyday practice? More generally how can professional power be challenged and how does the law address infringements of people's rights?

We shall now address each of these questions in turn.

How and why is the law changed?

The formal mechanism, whereby the law is changed, is best demonstrated by a diagram.

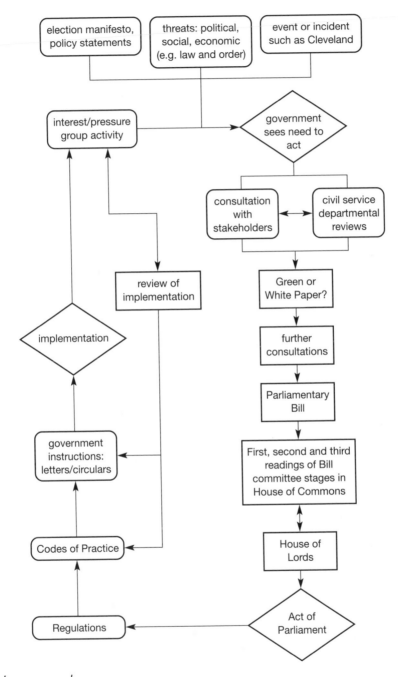

How laws are made

This is the process whereby the law is changed. Perhaps a more interesting question is why laws change. In this case example, why was the Children Act 1989 passed?

ACTIVITY 1.2

Why do you think the law changes? What reasons can you suggest for changes in legislation such as the Children Act 1989?

Spend a few moments reflecting on this. The answer is not quite as obvious as it may appear. Clearly one could simply say that the law was changed because Parliament said so, but this task is asking you to think about why Parliament changed the law.

Who do you think may have exerted pressure on MPs? Whose interests were served by the introduction of the Children Act 1989? What are the wider and broader issues here?

If you have already studied some social policy, you may find it slightly easier to answer the question in a systematic way by looking at changes at different levels and related to different ideologies. Even if you have not done so, you should still be able to suggest people and institutions that were key agitators for change.

We are not going to stray too much into the area of social policy, which is the academic discipline that tries to explain developments in the welfare state and social welfare legislation, but listed below are some suggestions as to why this Act was introduced. They are issues to think about and consider; there are no right and wrong answers here, simply matters of opinion. You'll find academics divided about the role law plays in social work, and whether it is always positive or beneficial. Listed at the end of this chapter are some suggestions for further reading in the area of social policy.

Reasons for the introduction of the Children Act 1989

- Individual MPs took up the plight of parents in Cleveland who considered themselves falsely accused of child abuse, and pressed for a full investigation which eventually took the form of a judicial inquiry (DHSS, 1988). Those MPs then pressed for changes in the law along the lines recommended by the Inquiry Report.

- Lawyers acting for the parents and others involved in child care court proceedings seized on the events in Cleveland as a demonstration of the inadequacy of child care legislation. They influenced Parliament directly and indirectly through pressure groups such as the Law Society.

- Social workers and other child protection professionals shared a common concern about the extent to which they are expected to intervene in families. They welcomed the Cleveland Report and the clarity that would be obtained by the Children Act 1989.

- Pressure groups representing the interests of children and families likewise seized the opportunity to press for 'reform' and they would have been able to provide other case illustrations of the need for change through the media and through contact with government departments and MPs.

All of these explanations, and there may well have been others that you could suggest, relate to people acting as individuals and groups. If we examine wider spheres of influences, it is possible to suggest additional factors operating.

- There was a broad ideological division between those who saw social workers and other child care professionals as always knowing what is in the best interests of the child, ranged against those who saw a need for the powers of professionals to be curtailed. The Children Act 1989 can be seen as part of the move to challenge professional power by involving the courts more in decision-making rights throughout the process of assessment.

- There may have been political differences, between those who argue that it is a duty of the state to promote the welfare of children and therefore there ought to be extensive legal powers available to ensure this, contrasted with those who see the law as infringing parents' rights and duties to look after their own children. Those in the latter category see the law as relevant only in a very narrow range of cases where child abuse has clearly been proven.

At an even broader level, the Children Act 1989 may demonstrate something about the relationship between the family and the state. Some would interpret this as reflecting economic changes that require families to take greater responsibility for themselves and a diminution of the role of the state. According to this argument, curbing welfare professionals' power is necessary in order to reduce public expenditure and dependency on government officials such as local authority social workers (Clarke, 1993; Fox-Harding, 1997). Debates about the welfare of children are complex, and arouse deep feelings in people. Some believe that the extent of child abuse is grossly exaggerated, and find it particularly difficult to accept that there is extensive sexual abuse of children. Conversely, some would argue that the extent of abuse is seriously underestimated. Media portrayals of social work tend to adopt one of these two extremes, whereas policymakers and legislators need to take a balanced view and this is achieved through requiring courts to make the key decisions.

If you are unfamiliar with the broader explanations of law and social work do look at the list under Further Reading at the end of this chapter for ways in which you can extend your knowledge and understanding.

There are a number of other potential explanations that may have occurred to you. Do not worry if you failed to identify those enumerated here. What matters is not the number that you correctly 'guessed' but that you can now see why the law needs to be involved in social work and what it is anticipated that the law will achieve.

What kinds of laws are there?

What kind of law is the Children Act 1989 and what types of law are there?

The difference between criminal law and civil law is familiar to most people. Criminal law is the law that provides sanctions or penalties for 'breaking' the law. It proscribes (prohibits) certain behaviour. If you steal, you commit a criminal offence. If you evade paying tax by not declaring something you know you must by law declare, you commit a criminal offence. If you break the speed limit, you commit an offence. All will result in some kind of punishment (penalty or 'sentence') – assuming you get caught, of course!

Civil law is about a legal wrong that results in harm to someone, for which they seek redress: recompense, compensation, matters put right, or some other course of action. It is not about punishment, so intention is often irrelevant. For example, you may unwittingly damage your neighbour's car when the tree in your garden falls on it. Or you may have caused injury to livestock by accidentally leaving a gate open, or failed to pay a debt. If you are libelled, you can claim for the damage done to your reputation and your career prospects. If you took lots of photocopies of this chapter without permission you would be in breach of copyright and the publishers could sue you (so be warned)! If parental action or inaction results in *significant harm* to a child the courts can take steps to address this – this is exactly what the Children Act 1989 says, so the Children Act 1989 is an example of civil law. If central or local government fail to carry out their duties properly, the courts can declare them to be in error. Likewise compensation can be ordered by the courts if an employer fails in their obligations to their employees or a trader sells faulty goods, and so on.

The differences are summarised in this table.

Table 1.1 *Criminal law and civil law*

	Criminal law	Civil law
Fundamental purpose	prosecution	redress
Referred to as	R *v* Smith	Smith *v* Smith Ayrshire *v* Smith Re C.S. (a child)
Outcome	sentence/punishment	judgment or resolution by agreement
Essentially about	'breaking the law', threat to society, intention (technically called mens rea) is important	tort – legal wrong, no intent need be proved, protection of vulnerable, defence from actions of powerful bodies
Cases decided on (burden of proof)	proof beyond reasonable doubt	balance of probabilities

In social work much of the law is civil law, and often it is implemented through tribunals rather than courts themselves. Tribunals are in effect specialist courts, dedicated to a specific purpose. For example, there are tribunals that hear appeals concerning registration of residential homes (Care Standards Tribunal) and Mental Health Review tribunals that decide on detention of patients under the Mental Health Act 1983.

One other key difference between laws is a difference between what is written down – which is what most people assume is 'the law' – and unwritten laws which are effectively principles and assumptions handed down over the years. These are the differences between statute law and common law.

Table 1.2 *Statute law and common law*

Statute law	Common law
written down laws: deal with specific topics (for example, local authority social services) or specific group of people (for example, the 'chronically sick and disabled'), can also be more general (for example, Race Relations Act 1976)	general unwritten rules which are commonly understood to be the law of the land: for example, the limits of the role of local authorities, rights of courts to intervene in what a local authority does, can fill the gaps between statutes
interpreted by reference to what the law actually says and how judges interpret what Parliament intended	interpreted by judges' reference to long-established unwritten rules and what has happened before
judges cannot change what statute law says but Parliament can	judges can change common law but statute law always overrides common law so ultimately authority lies with Parliament

written down
to what

Clearly the Children Act 1989 is an example of statute law, as is any law that is an Act of Parliament.

the law says.

ACTIVITY **1.3**

Below is a list of criminal laws that are statute; criminal laws that are common law-based; civil laws that are statute; and civil laws that are common law-based. They are all mixed up. Fit them into the matrix below so that you end up with examples of laws that fall into all of these categories.

Do bear in mind that statute laws sometimes fall into the categories of both criminal and civil law, since they can contain provision for criminal and civil offences. An example would be the Protection from Harassment Act 1997 which creates the offence of harassment (section 2) and potential for injunctions to prevent harassment (section 3). In this exercise opt for the category that primarily or mainly applies to that law.

Here is a list of laws you have to fit into the matrix below.

Chronically Sick and Disabled Persons Act 1970 *Criminal*

Once found not guilty of an offence by the court a defendant cannot usually be retried

People who are accused of crimes are assumed innocent until found guilty

Actively assisting someone to commit suicide is murder *Or criminal*

An employer's duty of care to employees

Failing to pay a TV licence fee *Civil*

Failing to pay rent *Civil*

All employees must be provided with a contract of employment

National Health Service and Community Care Act 1990

Crime and Disorder Act 1998

Family Law Act 1996

Spending money on a service which a local authority does not have statutory authority to provide means it is acting 'ultra vires'

Sexual Offences Act 2003

Care Homes Regulations 2001

Theft Act 1968

Here is the matrix. Fit the laws listed above into the category of law that best fits or describes that kind of law.

	Statute law	Common law
Criminal law		
Civil law		

You will find the answers in Exercise Answers, p143.

15

How does the law operate to set boundaries but without interfering too much in everyday practice?

We now need to explain some of the ways in which the law achieves its aims on a day-to-day basis. If you look at the Children Act 1989 you will find the law set out in very broad terms, with procedures outlined and guidelines, such as criteria by which courts decide cases, set out. For example, right at the start of the Act it tells us that in deciding children's cases the court must pay paramount consideration to the welfare of the child (section 1 Children Act 1989).

In this and other legislation, local authorities are given powers to provide services but the Act of Parliament itself does not necessarily say what those services should be. Part III Children Act 1989 empowers local authorities to provide services for children and parents, but does not make precise stipulations as to what the services might be. However, the Act does insist that certain categories of children are defined as being 'in need'; principally children with disabilities.

There are a variety of mechanisms for putting the flesh on the bones, for providing instruction and guidance in addition to the Act, yet without telling social workers what to do in every single case. These mechanisms are statutory instruments, Circulars and Codes of Guidance.

Statutory instruments

This is the general term for a variety of means of implementing laws. One such statutory instrument is the Schedules or Rules linked to a specific Act. These set out how an Act is to be implemented and are compulsory. For example, a social worker writing a report for a court explaining how a child came to be placed for adoption would follow the Family Procedure (Adoption) Rules 2005. Procedures adopted by tribunals about care standards in homes have to conform to the Protection of Children and Vulnerable Adults and Care Standards Tribunal Regulations 2002 (Care Standards Act 2000). The terms Rules, Regulations and Directions may be regarded as roughly interchangeable. They are all in effect the means (instruments) of implementing statutes (Acts of Parliament) and therefore must be obeyed in the same way as the Act itself must be.

They can be very important indeed. For example, the Mental Health Review Tribunal Rules set out the procedures for hearing cases where people are detained in hospital against their wishes and appeal for discharge. The Children Act 1989 Regulations cover a wide variety of matters, including placement of children and rules concerning allowing children on care orders to resume living at home with their parents (covered further in Chapter 4).

Circulars and Codes of Guidance

Implementation of an Act of Parliament can also be achieved through:

- circulars from the relevant department which set out how legislation should be implemented: these do not have the full force of law;

- Codes of Guidance or Codes of Practice: these are likewise models of good practice rather than enforceable directions.

There are quite a large number of Circulars or Letters issued by the Department of Health: so many in fact that they are listed separately on the Department's website (address at end of chapter). Their main purpose is to set out arrangements whereby law and policy can be translated into practice, so much of it may be financial. However, their significance for social work practice must not be underestimated. In community care a number of Circulars set out the precise kinds of services that local authorities may offer to individuals (see Chapter 5 for examples). Collaboration between health authorities and local authority social services departments is often facilitated and enabled by Circulars.

Some Codes of Practice give precise guidance regarding procedures to be adopted in certain kinds of circumstances. For example, the Mental Health Act 1983 delegates to the Code of Practice advice on procedures to follow regarding assessment of potential hospital patients, transport arrangements and similar detailed (but important) issues. Likewise the Police and Criminal Evidence Act 1984 refers to a Code of Practice (section 66) which sets out procedures for interviewing suspects, detaining people, taking samples and the like. Social workers called to an interview at a police station would need to know what the Code of Practice says. The advantage of a Code of Practice is that it can be amended from time to time without changing the Act of Parliament on which it is based and from which it derives its authority.

Whether a Code of Practice is obligatory depends on its status. Some are more compelling than others: for example, those specifically issued under Local Authority Social Services Act 1970 are strongest. Section 7(1) 1970 Act states that local authorities shall *act under the general guidance of the Secretary of State.* This has been taken to mean that local authorities should not depart from the 'statutory' guidance (i.e. guidance issued under section 7(1) 1970 Act) without good reason. So it is important to be clear when looking at a Circular as to whether it is issued under the authority of this Act: it will usually say so right at the start.

The law clearly cannot tell social workers what to do in every particular case. It is probably best to regard the law as a framework within which there may be a series of additional frameworks: the Circulars, Codes of Practice or whatever. The social worker's employer may offer additional policy guidance, but inevitably much depends on the assessment of the individual circumstances and the social worker's professionalism. To clarify this it may be worth setting out some key principles underlying the law and this relationship to social work.

Principles behind application of public law

- The group for whom services are provided needs to be identified, either specifically (for example, Chronically Sick and Disabled Persons Act 1970) or by interpretation (for example, the National Health Service and Community Care Act 1990 in practice applies to particular categories of people in need and the Children Act 1989 focuses on specific groups of children).

- If Parliament says action must be taken then the law applies to all, across the board. The duty cannot be refused on the grounds of difficulty, such as geographical isolation or lack of resources. The law also means what it says: for example, each local authority will have to appoint a Director of Children's Services when the Children Act 2004 is fully implemented (section 18 Children Act 2004). Duties cannot be delegated to another department although, if the law allows, services may be provided by other agencies, including those in the independent sector.

Children Act 1989 | S18 Duty band

- There is a very sharp distinction between mandatory and permissive powers. In everyday language mandatory means must, permissive means may. In fact, the law rarely makes the provision of specific services as such mandatory, preferring to make provision of information about services compulsory (as in Chronically Sick and Disabled Persons Act 1970 and National Health Service and Community Care Act 1990). Permissive powers are important since without these, local authorities would not be able to do anything. A local authority needs to be empowered to act since local authorities can only act when and where the law says it can. This contrasts with the position of individuals who are free to do whatever they wish unless the law says that they may not. In short, local authorities can do nothing unless the law says they can (otherwise they are acting *ultra vires*, beyond powers). Individuals can do what they want unless the law says they cannot.

- Furthermore, social work providers must offer services and exercise their powers (if they have powers established by law), in accordance with anti-discrimination legislation. In Britain, this legislation has until recently only covered three areas: gender or sex discrimination, racial discrimination and disability discrimination. However, age discrimination in employment is now covered by regulations (Employment Equality (Age) Regulations 2006), as is sexual orientation, whilst legislation concerning religious discrimination and stirring up *religious hatred* (Part 2 of the Equality Act 2006; Racial and Religious Hatred Act 2006) awaits implementation – although in the meantime it should be noted that ethnic discrimination (that might apply to the term Jewish, for example) may be covered under the Race Relations Act 1976 and Public Order Act 1986.

It is not intended to cover anti-discriminatory legislation in detail in this book. You may be surprised to learn that much of this does not directly address everyday social work practice. This is simply explained. Social work legislation is essentially positive action directed towards groups who are often disadvantaged or discriminated against, such as people with disabilities. By contrast, anti-discrimination legislation in Britain primarily provides for sanctions against people or bodies who 'unlawfully' discriminate against someone. Cases are, with a few exceptions, confined to individual people who would claim to be the victims of discrimination. Employment has historically been the main focus. Legislation in Britain, in contrast to other countries, places the responsibility on the claimant to prove they were discriminated against, rather than offering a general obligation on all employers, for example, to treat people fairly.

However, the tide now appears to be turning. The Race Relations (Amendment) Act 2000 requires public bodies to work towards the elimination of unlawful discrimination and promote equality of opportunity and good relations between different racial groups. The Equality Act 2006, when fully implemented, will require the new Commission for Equality and Human Rights to encourage and support the 'development of a society in which people's ability to achieve their potential is not limited by prejudice or discrimination, there is respect for and protection of each individual's human rights, there is respect for the dignity and worth of each individual, each individual has an equal opportunity to participate in society, there is mutual respect between groups based on understanding and valuing of diversity and on shared respect for equality and human rights' (section 3 Equality Act 2006).

Much of this accords with key principles and values of social work, with its emphasis on anti-discrimination principles and anti-oppressive practice (Dalrymple and Burke, 1995; Thompson, 2001). Exactly how the new Commission will set about its task remains to be seen.

C H A P T E R   S U M M A R Y

This chapter set out a number of reasons as to why the law is important in social work. It was suggested that the law should be seen in a positive light, setting the framework within which social work operates. It then offered a case example of a major legislative change that took place in Britain in the late 1980s, namely the Children Act 1989. This resulted indirectly from the events in Cleveland where social workers were accused of acting over-zealously. As a consequence, the judicial inquiry into events in Cleveland set out many of the key principles that are now enshrined in the Children Act 1989. Among these is the accountability of social workers to the law, and as you will see in Chapter 7 the courts play a key role in this.

The chapter then went on to consider the way in which laws are passed, and raised for consideration the issue of why the law changes. You may wish to read further on this, and will certainly be expected to do so if your social work training includes social policy.

You were then introduced to different ways of categorising legislation, and the different ways in which legislation is enacted through statutory instruments and guidance. The chapter concluded with reference to the principles that underpin the operation of public law in Britain: public law meaning the law that concerns the operation of public bodies and the relationship between the state and the individual. This then brings us full square into the ambit of human rights, which is where the next chapter starts.

FURTHER READING

To understand the purpose of law and law in context, it is essential to have some knowledge of social policy in relation to social work. One of the following will help.

Adams, R (2002) *Social policy for social work.* Basingstoke: Palgrave.

Alcock, P, Erskine, A and May, M (eds) (2003) *The student's companion to social policy* (2nd edition). Oxford: Blackwell.

Fox-Harding, L (1997) *Perspectives in Child Care Policy* (2nd edition). London: Longman.

Lavalette, M and Pratt, A (2005) *Social policy: theories, concepts and issues* (3rd edition). London: Sage.

WEBSITES

To keep up-to-date with developments the following websites can be recommended:

Commission for Equality and Human Rights: **www.cehr.org.uk/**

Department for Education and Skills: **www.dfes.gov.uk/childrenandfamilies/**

Department of Health: **www.doh.gov.uk/**

Learning Matters: **www.learningmatters.co.uk/**

Legislation including statutory instruments: **www.opsi.gov.uk/legislation/uk.htm**

Ministry of Justice: **www.justice.gov.uk/**

Chapter 2
Human rights

Introduction

This chapter explores the notion of rights as they apply to social work, focusing on 'human rights'. Here we will be primarily concerned with some very basic rights that have become adopted internationally and apply to the British legal and social welfare system. Leading on from this, the chapter summarises the various ways in which service users can challenge the decisions of social workers and local authorities in the courts. This is a key element in empowering individuals who feel they have not been fairly treated by people who are meant to be helping them or providing services for them. By reading this chapter and completing the associated exercises, you will be developing your basic understanding of how the law operates and what people's rights are.

In this chapter we will be looking at ways in which human rights are recognised by the law in Britain, focusing specifically on the impact of human rights related legislation on social work. The scene is set by a discussion of human rights generally, distinguishing between the various United Nations conventions or declarations and the European Convention on Human Rights since before pursuing basic human rights cases applicants need to pursue legal remedies in the UK. There is then a discussion on rights of redress under UK law. This leads on to a consideration of the Human Rights Act 1998 setting out the rights of redress this offers. The discussion then ranges more widely into the relationship between social work service users and the law, using as an example the debate about mental health legislation. This raises major ethical questions concerning the right of the state to intervene in the personal lives of individuals perceived to be dangerous yet where no offence has been committed. The chapter concludes by illustrating other areas of social work where the European Convention may have some influence, highlighting some cases which have already attracted our attention.

What are human rights?

Any exposition of human rights has to start by posing the very basic question: what are human rights?

ACTIVITY 2.1

Either on your own or in a small group, answer the following questions:

What do we mean when we talk about human rights?

What are the most important human rights?

Do not read on yet unless you want the answer.

When we talk about human rights there are a number of features that make them distinctive:

- they seem to refer to basic, fundamental needs;
- they should be universal, that is apply to everyone;
- they are essentially protective, ways in which individuals are protected against the power of the state or from each other;
- they are quite general;
- yet they have to be attainable regardless of resources;
- they are unconditional, everyone gets them, they are not 'earned'.

Your list may not coincide exactly with this, and when asked to decide the most important human rights, people are unlikely to be in complete agreement. Nevertheless, most lists of basic human rights include reference to:

- some kind of right to life;
- some reference to personal respect (no arbitrary arrest, law applied equally to all, and associated rights);
- some basic legal rights, such as a fair trial, due legal process;

- prohibition on torture;

- prohibition of slavery;

- some kind of rights to freedom of expression and belief.

Something you will have learned from this exercise is that it is not as easy as one might think. It is very tempting to talk about rights at a secondary level, such as entitlement to services and rights to participate in decision-making, and forget the prior requirement regarding the rights of people to participate in society more generally, and the rights to be treated equitably by the law. We take it for granted that people are no longer slaves, for example. Some of the difficulty may arise precisely from the fact that in Britain these basic rights are simply assumed: taken for granted and therefore unconsciously overlooked. However, there is no room for complacency and as we shall see in this chapter there are some fundamental principles concerning basic rights that may indeed conflict with current or intended laws in the UK.

Before exploring this we need to say a bit more about why we need human rights and where they come from.

The origins of human rights legislation lie in the aftermath of the Second World War. In order to prevent the recurrence of the atrocities that occurred during that war, countries of the world came together to form the United Nations and passed the United Nations Convention on Human Rights in 1948, consisting of 30 Articles and a number of related subsequent covenants (Brayne and Broadbent, 2002, pp68–72). This has not been adopted by all countries, and is not a code of law as such. Hence it is not possible to complain to the courts that action in a particular case breaches the Declaration on Human Rights – it is not incorporated into the law in that sense. Instead the Convention operates at a wider level. There are Conventions and Declarations made under the auspices of the United Nations that offer a kind of benchmark by which countries can be examined for the extent to which they comply with basic human rights. One of the best-known of these is the United Nations Convention on the Rights of the Child (1989). Every five years there are reports on policy changes and practices in each country by an international team appointed by the UN. This may be very effective in focusing publicity on certain policies, for example in the UK this has brought under scrutiny the policy of detaining 12–14-year-olds in custody (see Chapter 6), but it does not offer redress in individual cases.

There are certain other United Nations Declarations worth noting which operate in a similar fashion covering areas such as the rights of the disabled (1974) and elimination of discrimination against women (1981).

Essentially it is signing up to these Conventions and Declarations that is of significance; being in effect commitments of intent concerning legislation and policy. There are some other conventions that do have greater effect on individual cases: for example, there is a convention on torture that includes the power to investigate cases and, of course, there is a mechanism for hearing accusations of crimes against humanity in international courts at The Hague.

Of more immediate impact on individual cases is the European Convention on Human Rights. This was originally drawn up in 1950 but only in 1965 did Britain allow its citizens to petition the European Court. At this point it is important to make one point absolutely clear, since it is the cause of much confusion in the media. The European Convention on Human Rights is nothing, absolutely nothing, to do directly with the European Union. The European Union is essentially an economic partnership. Quite separately and apart from this economic partnership, a far greater number of countries in Europe agreed to forge a political alliance, the Council of Europe, whereby they would agree that certain basic rights would be granted to all individuals in all member countries. There are currently 46 members of the Council of Europe. It is this Council of Europe that formulated the European Convention on Human Rights and implements it through the European Court.

Although the UK government agreed to acknowledge the principles of the European Convention on Human Rights, until October 2000 there was no possibility of arguing in UK courts that an individual case breached the Convention. Instead, having exhausted all legal remedies in the UK, individuals could then complain to the European Court – in effect taking the UK government to court. The position was changed by the Human Rights Act 1998 which incorporated the European Convention into UK law. It does this in two ways. First it declares that all laws passed from 1998 onwards will in principle comply with the European Convention on Human Rights, although there is provision for exemptions (for example, a partial opt-out to Article 5 to enable counter-measures in cases of alleged terrorism to be adopted). Secondly it gave the courts the power to adjudicate by reference to the Convention so that in individual cases people could argue that there had been a fundamental breach of their human rights. This naturally applies to decisions made in accordance with all legislation, including legislation that was passed prior to 1998; in this case it may be that the court has to declare that part of the legislation itself is not compatible with the Convention.

Two limitations worth noting are that the Human Rights Act 1998 applies to public bodies, not to private individuals, or to all voluntary organisations. This may be a major obstacle in some cases, as we shall see in Chapter 5 (Cheshire Home case). The second limitation is that before appealing to the courts on European Convention on Human Rights grounds, applicants must attempt all other possible legal remedies. Only when someone has made every attempt to persuade the public body to their point of view can they then apply to the courts. The next section explains this in more detail.

How are infringements of people's rights challenged? How can decisions be challenged?

It is important to answer this in a general sense because it helps us to understand the role of courts in relation to local authorities and other service providers. In Chapter 1 we explored the differences between statute law and common law. One element of common law is the traditional role of the courts in protecting an individual against the arbitrary use of power, against the misapplication of the law by public bodies. The origins of this role are lost in the mysteries of time yet they have great contemporary significance, for the High Court derives from common law its powers to overrule public bodies and tell them that their interpretation of the law is wrong.

However, before service users can rush to the courts they need to be aware of three key principles:

- courts will intervene only if there is evidence of unjust treatment or mistaken interpretation of statute law;

- generally, courts won't make decisions for local authorities or government — they will simply say that a decision is wrong in law for a particular reason, with the implication that the public bodies will then correct this;

- complainants must explore *all other avenues* first.

What might these other avenues be?

Complaints procedures

The first obvious step, if someone is dissatisfied, is to complain. In the case of community care, for example, the National Health Service and Community Care Act 1990 provides for specific procedures for making and determining complaints. Other service provision may not be regulated by specific Acts, but service providers will generally have to offer robust complaints procedures in order to comply with service level agreements (that is, a formal contract between the local authority and the provider, essential in order that the provider acting as agent delivers a service consistent with the commissioner's responsibilities).

Maladministration and injustice

In the case of public bodies complaints of maladministration may be referred to:

- the Parliamentary and Health Service Ombudsman for England (website address at end of chapter), who deals with complaints about maladministration by government departments and the National Health Service, probably of most relevance to social work in hospitals and Care Trusts;

- the Local Government Ombudsman (Commissioner for Local Administration in England, website address at end of chapter) who deals with local authorities who employ social workers in their social services departments and children's services;

- in Wales the Public Services Ombudsman for Wales, who deals with all complaints regarding the work of public bodies (Public Services Ombudsman (Wales) Act 2005).

The ombudsman may only investigate injustice caused by maladministration. The complainant has to demonstrate that they suffered injustice through misapplication of procedures or lack of care over their application or something similar. Specifically *excluded* are matters of policy and allocation of resources. Inconsistency in the application of policy and procedures would be considered for adjudication, but not the actual principles and policies themselves. If the ombudsman's report goes against the local authority, the local authority has power to pay compensation but the commissioner's decision is *not* legally binding on the local authority.

Civil action for damages

If an individual has suffered damage or loss as a consequence of someone else's actions, they may wish to sue for damages in the civil court. To do this they would have to establish that some kind of civil legal wrong (technically a 'tort') occurred; for example, if a service user fell over an obstacle carelessly left around, or if someone alleged that they were injured or neglected as a result of the service provider failing to employ sufficient trained staff.

Having explored these remedies, what might service users expect of the courts?

Essentially courts have powers of judicial review and are required to interpret the European Convention as it applies to UK law.

Judicial review

Courts might be invited to order local authorities or other bodies to act (mandamus) or not to act (prohibition) in certain ways, but note that judicial review concerns the process by which the local authority arrived at its decision, not the actual decision itself.

Judicial review can now also consider the law itself as well as decisions made under the law and determine whether or not they comply with the European Convention on Human Rights. If the law and associated decisions are not compatible with the Convention, courts make a declaration of incompatibility and refer the matter back to Parliament. This obviously may offer little in the short term but in the long run can have very considerable consequences. In the meantime the assumption is that public bodies will offer some kind of compensation, recompense or redress.

European Court

Ultimately having proceeded through all UK administrative procedures and through the courts, the applicant has the right to appeal to the European Court of Human Rights itself. This can adjudicate when all UK procedures have been exhausted and when it is considered that there has been a specific breach of the European Convention on Human Rights.

Yet it is no good having rights unless we know what they are, so in the next two sections we explore the kinds of basic rights implemented in Britain through the Human Rights Act 1998.

Human Rights Act 1998 and the European Convention on Human Rights

There are some misconceptions and misunderstandings about this Act. It does not provide a means for overriding existing legislation. It does not allow the courts to 'strike down' legislation in the way that the Supreme Court can in interpreting the US Constitution. It does not apply penalties to public bodies that breach the Convention, preferring compensation instead. It does not apply to everyone, for as we have already seen, it may not apply to voluntary organisations.

So what then are the principles underlying the Human Rights Act 1998?

- It provides an avenue for redress in the UK courts for an individual who believes that their Convention rights have been breached and they have been affected by this. The second statement is important as it prevents purely academic complaints. It also disallows 'class actions' whereby large groups of people as a body can complain and claim damages.

- It requires public bodies in all that they do to act in accordance with the Convention and face claims for compensation if they do not.

- It requires the courts to take heed of the Convention when interpreting legislation. This applies to all courts at all levels. If the legislation itself appears to be incompatible with the Convention, then courts refer this back to Parliament.

- Parliament committed itself to passing legislation after 1998 that was compatible with the Convention but the Convention is not absolute, and there may be occasions in which Parliament exempts parts of particular statutes from the Convention, knowing the consequences of this.

- Interpretation of law applies to all kinds of law, criminal and civil, and all aspects of work carried out by public authorities. So it could apply to someone accused of an offence, or someone asking for 'judicial review' of the decision by a public body.

From this it would seem that the Human Rights Act is very wide-ranging, yet the Act itself is comparatively short. This is because it refers to the European Convention as the source of its authority.

Yet we still haven't answered the fundamental question: what are these Convention rights? Indeed, what are people's basic rights?

You may think you know some of the European Convention on Human Rights already, so now is the opportunity to put your knowledge to the test.

ACTIVITY 2.2

Either on your own or in a small group answer the following questions:

- *What areas do you think are covered by the European Convention on Human Rights?*

- *Which of the Convention Rights are most likely to be relevant to social work service users?*

The answers to these questions are in Exercise Answers, pp143–145.

Applying the European Convention on Human Rights benchmark

Let's look at some examples of recent cases where people have successfully used the convention either in courts in Britain or in the European Court itself. The cases are illustrative in order to show the kinds of issues the courts have legitimately considered and are not meant to cover the whole range – that would be quite a task.

Before looking at the examples, a word about citation of case law.

Where a case is reported, the convention is that the name of the person who initiated the legal action (the applicant, formerly referred to as the plaintiff) comes first followed by *v* for versus (often said as 'and') and the name of the respondent (defendant), who in European court cases might be a national government. Then follows the source: the published law reports such as *All England Law Reports* (All ER), *Family Law Reports* (FLR), Court of Appeal (CA) and the number of the case. Instead of the law report reference, in the case of European Court cases (ECHR) there may be a specific date, so that the case can be accessed through the court's internet site, or it may simply be unreported, which means it is not published as such – although people who were there know what happened of course. There are examples of each of these forms of citation in the following paragraphs, which provide brief summaries of cases that may be of general interest.

In each case, you are not told immediately which Convention Article has been breached so you may like to try to work this out for yourself before reading to the end of the case example. Cases of more specific application appear in other chapters and particularly important cases may well be putting in another appearance.

CASE STUDY

In January 2003 the European Court gave judgment about the use of public surveillance CCTV equipment (Peck v United Kingdom, ECHR 28 January 2003). The complainant, in a very depressed state of mind in the mid-1990s, had attempted suicide in a public place. His actions were filmed on closed-circuit television at the time and the police were called, took him for medical attention and he recovered. Subsequently the videotape of the suicide attempt was used on television, broadcast regionally and nationally, to extol the effective use of closed-circuit TV in public places. A picture was also used in a newspaper. Advertising CCTV merits in this way was deemed objectionable since it was done without consent, and the complainant persuaded the European Court that this was a breach of Article 8, the right to privacy, going well beyond what can be justified in the public interest.

The Appeal Court confirmed a ruling that the UK government's policy, introduced in 2002, of denying benefits to those who failed to claim asylum as soon as practicable was a breach of the European Convention on Human Rights. The denial of state support to late applicants for asylum (section 55 of the Nationality, Immigration and Asylum Act 2002) would in effect leave them destitute, potentially damaging their health and safety, and was therefore incompatible with Convention Article 3 (inhuman treatment) (CA 18 March 2003).

In a case concerning a housing tenancy the court agreed that the refusal to allow someone who was in a homosexual partnership to succeed to a particular tenancy seemed to be a contravention of the Convention since the succession would have been allowed in the case of a married couple (Mendoza v Ghaidan [2003] 2 WLR 478). Likewise the Liverpool County Court confirmed in 2002 that this should also apply to the definition of nearest relative in the Mental Health Act 1983 (SSG v Liverpool City Council, unreported, 22 October 2002). Both these cases were held to be contrary to Article 14 concerning discrimination.

CASE STUDY (CONTINUED)

The tragic Bland case concerned a victim of the Hillsborough disaster and whether life support equipment could be turned off where a person was in a vegetative state and unlikely to recover (Airedale National Health Service Trust v Bland [1993] AC 789). Here the courts held that the obligation to preserve life is not absolute, and specifically in some circumstances it is acceptable to discontinue treatment.

In another tragic case, a teacher shot a school student's father (Osman v United Kingdom [2000] 29 EHRR 245). This followed a period of harassment which, it was argued, the police knew about, but from which they failed to protect the family. It was alleged that the police were negligent in this regard, and therefore the state had failed in its basic duty of protection of the right to life (Article 2). The court rejected this argument, referring to operational choices, priorities and resources that confronted the government and the police.

Dianne Pretty wanted the courts in Britain to guarantee that her husband would not be prosecuted if he helped her to commit suicide. The courts in Britain refused to do this, arguing that assisting suicide was manslaughter and people did not have the right to die under the European Convention, a decision confirmed by the European Court (Pretty v United Kingdom ECHR 29 April 2002).

In a case where a local authority took the serious step of removing a child from her mother shortly after birth, the European Court ruled that this action was not justified by relevant and sufficient reasons. It could not be regarded as having been necessary in a democratic society for the purpose of safeguarding the child and therefore breached Article 8, right to family life (P, C and S v the United Kingdom, ECHR 16 July 2002).

The trial of two boys accused of the murder of Jamie Bulger was held in an adult court and therefore, according to the European Court, in unsuitable surroundings where they were unable to participate effectively. Also the European Court held that there was political interference in the sentence by the Home Secretary; sentences must be judicial (V v United Kingdom, ECHR 6 December 1999). This case concerned interpretation of Article 6, the right to a fair trial, and has led to a major review of the trial setting for young people (see Chapter 6 for reference to the Lord Chief Justice's ruling on this). It has also meant that the Lord Chief Justice will in future decide the actual length of time offenders remain in custody if this is indeterminate.

Two cases concerned the physical punishment of children. In the first (Costello-Roberts v UK [1993] 19 EHRR 112) corporal punishment of children in schools was held to be illegal (by 1993 it had been formally banned in state schools but permitted in independent schools). The second case concerned a step-father who caned his step-son and was prosecuted, but escaped conviction in the UK criminal courts because he could argue, using case law interpretation of the Children and Young Persons Act 1933, that the assault was justified as reasonable chastisement. The European Court rejected this and declared that in this instance the state had failed to protect a child from inhuman or degrading punishment (Article 3) by allowing the step-father this defence (A v UK [1998] FLR 959 UK). Subsequently the Children Act 2004 (section 58) withdrew the defence on which the step-father relied in this case.

CASE STUDY (CONTINUED)

A former resident of children's homes and community homes claimed the right of access to all records the local authority held about them, including adoption records (Gaskin v UK [1986] 12 EHRR 36). This right was refuted by the courts which declared there had been no breach of Article 10. Since this case, there have been substantial amendments to the law, to such an extent that in effect service users do have the right to see written and electronic records (Data Protection Act 1998), but not adoption records (although there is provision even for this in the Adoption and Children Act 2002).

Of particular significance for social work is the 'Bedfordshire' case that has been proceeding through the courts in Britain for several years (this case has different citations according to the court that heard it, but it is the same case). The case concerned the alleged lack of action by a local authority in protecting children. Whilst there was no fundamental dispute that children in this case had been left too long with their family and should have been the subjects of care proceedings much earlier, the issue that the courts faced was whether this lack of action constituted a legitimate legal claim for compensation for the children arising from the local authority's failure to protect them. In 1995 the House of Lords decided that local authorities should be immune from legal action since otherwise it will be an enormously difficult task for any local authority to carry out its child protection functions without being sued (X (minors) v Bedfordshire County Council [1995] 3 All ER 353). However the European Court disagreed, and awarded the children damages for the abuse. The court considered that here that had been a breach of two Articles. The first is Article 3 – as a consequence of the local authority's failure the children had suffered inhuman treatment. The European Court also declared the English legal system to be failing its obligations under Article 13 because it did not allow the children to sue the local authority, thereby denying them an effective remedy.
(Z and others v the United Kingdom [2001] 2 FLR 612)

These summaries can do no more than give you a flavour of the kinds of issues raised in human rights cases that may have some relevance, directly or indirectly, to social work. If you are especially interested in this area, further cases relevant to health and social care may be found through the Department of Health website (address at end of this chapter) or in Brayne and Broadbent (2002). At this point we turn to the use of the European Convention on Human Rights as a benchmark for legislation, using as a case example proposed amendments to mental health law. The reasons for this are twofold:

- it will demonstrate the principles underpinning the European Convention on Human Rights as it applies to one key issue, the liberty of the individual;

- this will facilitate an analysis of challenges posed by trying to balance people's rights to decide for themselves, and the need to protect them where they may be unable to make sound decisions

In making these considerations, Parliament now needs to ensure that new legislation satisfies the requirements of the European Convention on Human Rights, so it is important to know what these are. It needs to be emphasised that the case study relates to *proposed* legislation – not current law. The proposals were set out in draft Mental Health Bills published in 2004 and 2006 (Department of Health, 2004a; Department of Health, 2006a).

Mental health, the European Convention on Human Rights and persons of unsound mind

So what are the principles governing the way the European Convention on Human Rights addresses mental health laws?

First, we need to identify the relevant parts of the European Convention on Human Rights.

Article 5 covers rights to liberty, which has self-evident relevance to the detention of people with mental health problems.

Article 2, the right to life, is partially relevant as it requires governments to take appropriate steps to safeguard the lives of people within its jurisdiction.

Article 8 is relevant in respect of the rights of nearest relatives and access to information.

Article 3 concerns treatment, specifically stipulating that it must not be *inhuman or degrading*.

Article 5

Article 5(1) grants a general right to *liberty* and *security of person*. There are obvious exceptions to this as an absolute principle, for example, relating to people who are convicted of criminal offences, or are suspected of having done so. Exemption 5(1)(e), though, concerns the detention of *persons … of unsound mind*.

The European Court has considered a number of cases of people apparently of *unsound mind* and thereby established some general principles and safeguards. The key case concerned Dutch law and procedures for assessment and detention (Winterwerp v The Netherlands [1979] 2 EHRR 387). Through this case, the European Court laid down that in order for detention to be lawful under Article 5(1)(e) three conditions must be met (except in emergency):

1. a true mental disorder must be established before a competent authority on the basis of objective medical expertise;

2. the mental disorder must be of a kind or degree warranting compulsory confinement;

3. the validity of continued confinement depends on the persistence of such a mental disorder.

The first principle clearly implies that there must be a prior medical assessment of mental disorder before someone can be detained.

The second principle has been clarified to refer to compulsory confinement somewhere which is appropriate for the detention and where treatment is offered. Detaining someone in a prison psychiatric wing for a lengthy period was considered a breach of the convention as no medical or therapeutic treatment was offered (Aerts v Belgium [1998] 29 EHRR 50).

Courts have also had to consider whether in order to qualify for detention the potential patient has to suffer from a condition that is *treatable*. Consideration of various cases has stretched the principle to encompass the need to protect the public even where it is unlikely that treatment will bring about any improvement (Anderson, Doherty and Reid *v* the Scottish Ministers and the Advocate General for Scotland, Times Law Report, 21 June 2000).

The third principle, validity of continued confinements, is relevant to Mental Health Review Tribunal discharges where someone is no longer mentally *disordered* to the extent that confinement is necessary. Article 5(4) is the right to challenge the lawfulness of detention. In practice this must mean a review of the decisions to detain within a reasonable period: two months was too long (E *v* Norway [1994] 17 EHRR 30). The principles applicable here were brought together in a German case (Megyeri *v* Germany [1993] 15 EHRR 584):

1. detainees are entitled to periodic reviews by court or tribunal;

2. procedures must be *of judicial character*;

3. detainees must either be present or speak through a representative, with special safe-guards to protect people not capable of speaking for themselves;

4. detainees do not have to take the initiative.

Application of these principles led the British courts to conclude that sections 72 and 73 of the Mental Health Act 1983 were unlawful as they seemed to place the burden on the patient to prove that the conditions of detention were no longer met (R (H) *v* London North and East Region Mental Health Review Tribunal (Secretary of State for Health intervening) [2001] 3 WLR 512).

However, courts have taken the view that the periodic reviews by a tribunal do not imply an absolute right to be discharged if the tribunal agrees. In one case, the Mental Health Review Tribunal ordered a patient's discharge from compulsory detention in hospital, but this could not be carried out because of lack of availability of discharge resources. The patient argued that this meant he had to stay in detention despite the tribunal ruling, and therefore his right to freedom had been curtailed (R *v* Mental Health Review Tribunal, Torfaen County Borough Council and Gwent Health Authority, *ex parte* Russell Hall [2000] 1 WLR 1323). In another case, the discharge plans were thwarted by the lack of availability of a forensic psychiatrist, but the patient failed to persuade the court that this violated the right to liberty principle (R *v* Camden and Islington Health Authority, *ex parte* K [2001] EWCA Civ 240).

Article 2

Article 2 states that everyone's right to life shall be protected by law. This is qualified by certain rights in relation to people who commit offences and in public order situations, but in mental health the European Court has emphasised that, in addition to refraining from the intentional and unlawful taking of life, governments are required to take appropriate steps to safeguard the lives of its citizens. This positive obligation is likely to apply to individuals who were receiving psychiatric services, particularly where detained in hospital under the Mental Health Act 1983, although there have been no specific cases concerning this yet. In

Britain, the Department of Health and the Welsh Assembly have declared that they are taking steps to reduce the numbers of suicides by people with mental health problems by setting targets or audit procedures. These are set out in the National Service Framework for Mental Health Standard (Department of Health, 1999) and the Revised Adult Mental Health National Service Framework and Action Plan for Wales (Welsh Assembly, 2005).

Article 3

Article 3 outlaws inhuman or degrading treatment which must, according to the European Court, attain a *minimum level of severity*, dependent on the circumstances of the case.

Not surprisingly there have been several complaints under this Article relating to the treatment of mental health patients. Forcible administration of food and medication, together with use of handcuffs and a security bed, were not considered a violation of Article 3 if they were a *therapeutic necessity* (Herczegfalvy *v* Austria [1992] 15 EHRR 437). Likewise, the European Court will not concern itself with the side-effects of medication, refusing to accept that this is relevant to consideration of inhuman treatment (Grare *v* France [1993] 15 EHRR CD 100). So long as the treatment is therapeutically necessary, the convention is not considered to apply. However, a violation of Article 3 did occur when a prisoner suffering a diagnosed mental illness had his request to be released on licence refused yet continued to be detained without medical treatment or supervision (Jean-Luc Rivière *v* France [2006] ECHR 11 July 2006).

Article 8

Article 8(2) states that there shall be no interference with the exercise of the right to privacy, family life, home and correspondence *except such as is in accordance with the law and is necessary in a democratic society in the interests of national security, public safety or the economic well-being of the country, for the prevention of disorder of crime, for the protection of health or morals, or for the protection of the rights and freedoms of others.*

Under this Article, Nearest Relative definitions (section 26 Mental Health Act 1983) have been successfully challenged, since the Act allows no leeway: Nearest Relative is defined by law not by patient's choice, and the Nearest Relative has considerable power under the Act (for example, to order the patient's discharge). The impossibility in the Act of accommodating the patient's desire to change the identity of her Nearest Relative was considered a violation of Article 8 (JT *v* United Kingdom [2000] 1 FLR 909).

The challenge of new mental health legislation

In June 2002, the Department of Health published a draft Mental Health Bill, proposals to 'reform' mental health law. This followed in the wake of publicity generated by cases where members of the public had been injured or, in isolated cases, killed by people with a history of mental health problems (the most well-known case being that of the murder of Jonathan Zito by Christopher Clunis, a man diagnosed with paranoid schizophrenia, in December 1992).

The Mental Health Bill proved to be very controversial, and did not become law. It was reintroduced for debate in the 2004–2005 parliamentary session, but ran into a great deal of controversy, and again failed to become law. A revised Bill was then introduced in the 2006–2007 parliamentary session.

Here we will focus on the key elements of the proposed legislation, particularly on the 2004 Bill in order to demonstrate what was so controversial. You can find the details of what was covered in the 2004 proposals on the Department of Health website (see websites at the end of this chapter). The Mental Health Bill 2004 proposed:

- compulsory treatment for some *mentally disordered* people in the community;
- compulsory detention in hospital beyond 28 days to be authorised only by a Mental Health Tribunal;
- safeguards for patients who do not have capacity to understand or consent to treatment;
- a broader definition of mental disorder, extended to learning disabilities and possibly personality disorders;
- the social worker role in applying for admissions to be replaced by *approved mental health professional*;
- patients' powers to nominate a person to represent their interests;
- greater appeal rights to the Mental Health Tribunal;
- formalised care plans;
- changes in rules regarding discharge.

On the surface it would appear that these proposals are well intentioned and conform to the European Convention on Human Rights (and the government has declared that the new legislation should be consistent with the Convention). However, a number of objections have been raised.

ACTIVITY **2.3**

Looking back at the kinds of issues that have been brought before the European Court and bearing in mind these proposals, what general or specific objections do you think could be raised about the proposals? List as many as you can.

You may wish to look at a number of websites to find out more information about the government's proposals and the points raised by various advocacy organisations and service user groups about them. You will find the list of websites at the end of the chapter.

There was no expectation that you would cover all of the proposals. Indeed, there were such widespread objections to the proposals that it is difficult to be selective, but it would appear that the key areas where rights are most contentious and the debate most vigorous are as follows.

Compulsory treatment in the community

As we have seen, the European Court has not concerned itself with compulsory treatment in the community, leading to fears of a lack of court interest in this area.

Community treatment orders may mean that people are less inclined to accept any form of psychiatric treatment on the grounds that they are at risk of having this forced on them if they do not comply. There are, in addition, a large number of questions about the practicalities: for example, what happens if someone fails to turn up at a day centre? Who should force people to accept treatment or attend 'therapeutic' sessions? To what extent should the police be involved?

Role of tribunals

There would have to be more Mental Health Tribunals in order for UK procedures to conform to the principles laid down by the European Court (see discussion about Articles 5(1) and 5(4) above). This might divert financial and staff resources from front-line patient care.

Code of practice and principles for use of compulsion

There was very real concern that the principles for use of compulsion were much wider and therefore potentially open to abuse. Added to the broader definition of mental disorder, this might lead to a much more extensive use of complusion. Some considered that the consequences would be increased and unwarranted use of compulsion (see MIND website). The Royal College of Psychiatrists believed that people should not be compelled into treatment or hospital solely in order to prevent criminal behaviour.

Capacity to understand and consent

Under the Mental Health Act 1983 people who lacked capacity to consent but did not actively resist admission to hospital or treatment were classified as 'informal' patients and therefore not protected by the same safeguards as detained patients. Such 'informal' patients could be treated and possibly kept in hospital under common law, or so it was thought, and the 2004 Bill continued with this presumption. For in 1998 a British court decided that where someone does not have the capacity to agree or object to admission, but complies with being taken there, they may be kept in hospital 'informally' even if someone objects on their behalf (R v Bournewood Community and Mental Health NHS Trust, *ex parte* L (Secretary of State for Health and others intervening) [1998] 3 All ER 289).

However, the European Court in October 2004 ruled that this approach was not compatible with Article 5 of the Convention (HL *v* United Kingdom [2004] 40 EHRR 761) since using common law to detain someone in hospital was too aritrary and lacked sufficient safeguards. This effectively compelled a rethink about core assumptions that underpinned mental health legislation and led to a new Mental Health Bill being put forward in 2006, together with amendments to the Mental Capacity Act 2005 (see Chapter 5).

Broader definition of mental disorder

There is very real concern here that people with learning disabilities will be brought into the ambit of mental health legislation. This extends the remit of mental health legislation quite considerably and may even challenge the European Convention principle that liberty should only be restricted where someone is proven to be of *unsound mind*. The same applies to the proposed extension of legislation to people with 'personality disorders', a move actively opposed by the British Medical Association and other professional and service user groups.

The social worker role

Both the 2004 and 2006 Bills proposed substituting *approved mental health professionals* for social workers as approved applicants for patients' detention, thereby potentially broadening the scope for giving powers to non-social work professionals. Grave concern has been expressed at the lack of social care assessment as an integral part of the whole process and the significant reduction in the social work role generally.

Patients' powers to nominate advocates

This power had to be introduced to meet the objections to current legislation that arose in cases concerning definition of nearest relative (see discussion under Article 8 above) and also in the light of the passing of the Civil Partnership Act 2004. Generally this move has been welcomed, and clearly offers patients potentially more say in who should represent them. Some reservations remain about exactly what powers advocates would have and how an advocacy system would be financed. Also questions arise about advocates' rights of access to information.

More generally in relation to people's rights

Overall there appears to be an underlying assumption that people with mental health problems are dangerous. Many organisations have pointed out that there is no service user right to an assessment, and no entitlement to services as such. If you look up the websites listed at the end of this chapter you will see that there remain a number of issues of concern to professional and service users, which primarily revolve around the over-emphasis on control and compulsion, and disempowerment of service users themselves.

Conclusion

From this it will be seen that a number of important ethical and legal issues arise. They all centre on the issue of rights. To what extent should the state intervene in the lives of people who may not have committed a crime, yet may potentially pose a threat to themselves or to others? This is the crux of the matter. The European Convention offers some kind of guidelines, yet we can identify some deficiencies, especially in relation to compulsory treatment in the community. At the same time, we can see that in trying to adhere to the Convention there is a danger of overplaying the role of tribunals to the extent that resources for services may suffer. Yet we would have to concede that the Convention is important for, without it, there would be a real danger of the government or state simply deciding who was dangerous without allowing any possibility of independent review of such cases. The debate about the success of the Convention in promoting or constraining the rights of people with mental health problems is a very real and important one, which will continue for some time to come. At least by now the hope is that you can see how the Convention has an impact on UK law and social work practice, and also how it connects into major ethical debates and issues.

C H A P T E R S U M M A R Y

This chapter has explored the concept of rights in social work with special reference to the Human Rights Act 1998 that integrates the European Convention on Human Rights into everyday social work law and practice. You were asked to identify the fundamental rights that human beings share, and were then presented with an overview of the forms of redress to which service users are entitled in UK. This started with a summary of the legal processes whereby decisions made by public bodies might be challenged. The ultimate test lies with interpretation of the European Convention either in UK courts or ultimately in Strasbourg at the European Court. To demonstrate the operation of human rights in practice, the chapter then highlighted some specific examples of decisions made about basic rights that may have relevance to social work. We then focused on the example of mental health law and the European Convention, specifically its provisions for detention and control of people (of *unsound mind*) perceived to be a danger to themselves or to others. This led on to a discussion of recent proposals for changes in mental health legislation in England and Wales, and you were invited to assess these by reference to the European Convention. Some critical commentary made by a variety of organisations was then offered; this pointed to some key weaknesses in how the legislation proposed to respect people's rights and also hinted at a number of potential implications.

In the face of a volley of criticism, the government temporarily shelved attempts to change the law in 2002, and again in March 2005, but is obliged to press on with a reformulation of the law as current legislation does not conform to the European Covention in several respects. Whatever form new legislation eventually takes, you will now be in no doubt that it needs to be framed in a way that complies with the requirements of the European Convention on Human Rights. This principle of compatibility with the European Convention applies to all laws currently in force in the UK and, naturally, applies to all legislation and decision-making by public bodies in all other areas of social work.

The next chapter starts the specific examination of law as it relates to particular areas of social work, beginning with work with children and families. Yet again the issue of balancing people's rights with the obligations of the state will come to the fore, but now these will need to be examined in the context of children's rights.

FURTHER READING

If you are particularly interested in the example of mental health cited here as a demonstration of the European Convention on Human Rights in practice, you may like to look at one of the following which explores the issues much further than space permits here.

Fennell, P (1999) The third way in mental health policy: negative rights, positive rights and the convention. Journal of Law and Society 26, 103–127.

Johns, R (2005) Of unsound mind? Mental health social work and the European Convention on Human Rights. Practice 16(4), 247–259.

Prior, PM (2001) Protective Europe: does it exist for people with mental disorders? Journal of European Social Policy 11(1), 25–38.

WEBSITES

Afiya Trust, representing the interests of black and minority ethnic professionals and service users **www.afiya-trust.org/mentalhealth.htm**

British Association Social Workers: **www.basw.co.uk/**

British Medical Association: **www.bma.org.uk/ap.nsf**

Department of Health summary of human rights cases: **www.dh.gov.uk/PolicyAndGuidance/EqualityAndHumanRights/HumanRights/fs/en**

European Convention on Human Rights: **www.echr.coe.int/ECHR/EN/Header/Basic+Texts/Basic+Texts/The+European+Convention+ on+Human+Rights+and+its+Protocols/**

European Court judgments: **www.echr.coe.int/ECHR/**

Kings Fund: independent charity concerned with health and health information generally (lots of useful links to organisations and sources of information): **www.kingsfund.org.uk/**

Local government ombudsman for England: **www.lgo.org.uk/**

Mental Health Alliance, consortium of mental health voluntary organisations: **www.mentalhealthalliance.org.uk/**

Mental Health Bill 2004: **www.dh.gov.uk/assetRoot/04/08/89/14/04088914.pdf**

MIND: **www.mind.org.uk/News+policy+and+campaigns/Policy/ Mind+policy+on+revised+mh+bill.htm**

National Institute for Mental Health in England: **www.nimhe.org.uk/**

Parliamentary Joint Committee on mental health, commentary on 2004 proposals: **www.parliament.uk/parliamentarycommittees/jcdmhb.cfm**

Parliamentary and Health Service Ombudsman for England: **www.ombudsman.org.uk**

Public Services Ombudsman for Wales: **www.ombudsman-wales.org.uk/**

Sainsbury Centre for Mental Health, a charity concerned with the quality of life of people with severe mental health problems: **www.scmh.org.uk/wbm23.ns4/WebLaunch/LaunchMe**

SANE, mental health charity: **www.sane.org.uk/public_html/index.shtml**

Chapter 3
Children's rights and needs

Introduction

This chapter begins a two-part examination of the important relationship between children, their families, social work and the law. In this chapter, the focus is on children's basic needs and rights. This moves forward from the previous chapter where we looked at the basic human rights that everyone shares. Chief amongst these needs specific to children are education and the need to be looked after and supported during the process of growing up. One of the key concepts is that of working in partnership with parents. From the child's perspective, the law is important as it starts with their needs and then examines the most appropriate ways of meeting those needs, even if there is occasionally a conflict with some adults' perceptions of what those might be. In Chapter 4, we shall be concentrating more closely on legal arrangements when things go wrong: when families have what appear to be irreconcilable disputes, or when children need protection from *significant harm*.

The lengthy list of relevant occupational standards hints at the breadth of social work responsibilities in relation to children, as does the fact that there are two chapters devoted to this area. In this chapter we will be starting with some fundamental considerations of the position of children in society and within the legal system, before going on to consider some ways in which children's needs are met in the UK.

This chapter considers:

- the legal definition of childhood;

- the rights of children that are recognised internationally;

- meeting children's needs for education;

- supporting families and helping them to look after children;

- provision of substitute care when this is necessary for children;

- transition to adulthood.

What is a child?

You might think the answer to this question was pretty obvious, but bearing in mind that this is a book about the law and social work, how exactly would you define a child? After all, when we are talking about social arrangements to provide for the needs of children, we need to be clear from the outset exactly whose needs we are discussing. When we are talking about children's rights, we need to be able to say precisely to whom these rights apply.

ACTIVITY **3.1**

If you were asked to come up with a definition of a child, what would you say? Bear in mind that the definition has to withstand legal tests: it has to be consistent, applicable to everyone, readily understandable and potentially enforceable (that is, someone should be able to come along and say quite definitively that that person is a child whereas another person is not).

You should spend about ten minutes on this activity.

You may have started to approach this from the perspective of the vulnerability or dependence of certain human beings, but there are problems in applying this in the legal context.

A number of practitioners have pointed out that people with learning disabilities retain an apparently childlike capacity to conceptualise and relate to other people which, in some contexts, makes them quite vulnerable. Nevertheless the law cannot recognise this vulnerability since the law anchors its definitions on chronological age.

No matter how you approach the issue of defining childhood, inevitably for simplicity, you will probably have ended up with a definition based on age. However, what age? Would you recognise, formally and legally, a transition stage between childhood and adulthood? If so, at what age does this transition start and when does it finish? It is tempting to answer this by reference to physical growth and development, perhaps using puberty, the biological transition from childhood to young adulthood, as the marker. But this makes the issue more problematic, for puberty occurs at different ages in different young people, and so the outcome would certainly not be consistent. Consistency will only really be achieved by using biological age, which is easy to check (through birth certificates and other formal documentation) and indisputable.

So if age is the key factor, what age marks the end of childhood? Do we still wish to incorporate a formal transition period – for the sake of argument, something akin to adolescence?

Sociologists and historians (for example, Ariès, 1979) have pointed out that the age at which childhood ends varies considerably between different cultures and different time periods. Ariès points out that in France, along with a number of other European countries, for several centuries the convention was that no gender distinctions were made between children until comparatively late, sometimes up to the age of 7, when children suddenly lost their 'innocence'. In Britain, children in the nineteenth century were held fully responsible under the criminal law from the time they attained their eighth birthday. The age of criminal responsibility is now 10 in England and Wales, but this contrasts markedly with other countries.

Table 3.1 Age of criminal responsibility in other countries

Belgium	18
China	14
Egypt	15
France	13
Germany	14
India	7
Japan	14
Morocco	12
Nepal	10
Philippines	9
Poland	13
South Africa	7
Spain	16
Thailand	7
Turkey	11
UK (England and Wales)	10
UK (Scotland)	8
Ukraine	10
United States	7 (but variations between states)

Furthermore, if you look at the following table, you will see that there is not a great deal of consistency in ages at which children and young people are allowed to undertake certain activities in the UK.

Table 3.2 Ages at which activities become permissible (examples)

Age	Activity
13	Employment, although allowed at an even earlier age for theatrical performances and in agriculture
14	Hold a shotgun certificate
15	Watch 15 certificate films
16	Drive mopeds, consent to sexual activity, buy some alcohol to drink with meal, buy lottery tickets, join army or get married with parental consent
17	Drive car, purchase shotguns and firearms
18	Vote, marry, purchase alcohol, buy fireworks, use betting shop
21	Drive bus, adopt, be elected to Parliament

You may think that these are simply anomalies, but in fact it reflects a difficulty in framing the law so that it protects the vulnerability of young people whilst not being too oppressive. One example of this may be law regarding drinking alcohol: in certain USA states, the minimum age for buying alcoholic drinks is 21, whereas in the UK there is a debate about whether it should be lowered from 18. It may be this also reflects the fact that the law does not formally recognise adolescence. Adolescence is a psychological or sociological term, not a legal one. Where the law does make a distinction, most usually in criminal law, it uses the term *young persons* to refer to the in-between age, usually 14 to 17.

In the law which we are going to examine in this chapter and the next, the term 'children' has a slightly wider use than it does in everyday life. In the next section we look at the United Nations Convention on the Rights of the Child which regards children as all people under the age of 18, unless the law of a particular country states otherwise. The law in Britain makes education compulsory up until the end of the academic term or year in which the young person attains the age of 16. The Children Act 1989 has it both ways. In relation to 'private' proceedings, that is, court cases that do not concern local authorities or other public bodies, children are people under the age of 16. In relation to 'public' law and social services departments'/children's services authorities' responsibilities for providing services to children, children are people under the age of 18.

Sometimes the law does not insist on a chronological age, but allows professionals to make a judgment. One sensible example of this relates to consent to medical treatment and respecting confidentiality. If the law insisted that children only attained adult rights on their eighteenth birthday, this would mean that parents had absolute rights to determine whether and how children accepted medical treatment. This issue came to the fore in the case of Gillick (Gillick *v* West Norfolk and Wisbech Area Health Authority [1986] AC 112) where a parent tried to stop a family GP giving contraceptive advice and medical treatment to anyone in the family under 18. The decision in that case confirmed that having arbitrary age limits was artificial and quite inappropriate since it ignored the level of understanding and competence of individuals concerned to give consent. Therefore the judgment allows professionals to consider whether young people have sufficient competence to give informed consent, and if so, the young person's rights override those of the parent to object. In 2006 the courts confirmed this principle and extended it to young people's rights to confidentiality. In the Axon case (R (on the application of Axon) *v* Secretary of State for Health [2006] EWHC 37 Admin) the court rejected a mother's contention that she had the right to know if health care professionals proposed giving her children advice on sexual matters, including abortion. Guidelines asserting young people's independent rights to confidentiality did not conflict with parental rights under Article 8 of the European Convention on Human Rights. These judgments are important and exert considerable influence on social work and medical practice, although confidentiality is not an absolute, and can be overridden in cases of risk to health, safety or welfare (see Chapter 4).

Children's rights

In Chapter 2 we examined some basic fundamental human rights that people in the UK now expect to be respected by the law through the operation of the Human Rights Act 1998. We are now going to consider the specific and additional rights that children ought to have, over and above the rights accorded to adults. The next activity asks you to consider what you think these should be, so it might be advisable to look again at Chapter 2 if you cannot recall what basic human rights are.

ACTIVITY 3.2

Think about children you know of different ages. Think about children in different parts of the world. Think about children from different cultures and diverse backgrounds. Then write down what you think are the basic needs of all children.

You should spend about 15 to 20 minutes on this exercise. It may be helpful to undertake the exercise in a small group where you can share ideas and challenge each other about whether identified needs apply to all children.

It is more difficult than you may have assumed to think about basic needs, since, especially in the West, it is so easy to take basic necessities for granted. Let's see if your list of needs can be fitted into the following headings.

- Physical: under this heading we might include shelter in the form of some kind of home in which to live, sufficient food and water to survive, access to primary medical care that ensures survival, protection from harm.

- Developmental: access to food and water of sufficient quality to provide for growth and development, access to medical care that prevents disease and promotes growth, literacy to a sufficient level that ensures participation in society.

- Emotional: security (in all its forms, including freedom from oppression and persecution and identity), love and affection, respect as an individual.

The various countries of the world have attempted to codify children's basic needs and set out a charter of rights that is applicable to all countries. This codification is the United Nations Convention on the Rights of the Child. Before going any further, it is important to underline that this has not been adopted by the UK government as part of its legislative framework, so the United Nations Convention does not perform the same role as the European Convention on Human Rights in relation to the Human Rights Act 1998.

Furthermore, it should be noted that not all countries are signatories to the United Nations Convention, the most conspicuous non-signatory being the United States (the other is Somalia) (see website list at the end of the chapter for access to the full Convention).

Nevertheless the United Nations Convention is important for a number of reasons. First of all it sets out benchmarks by which countries ought to judge their own legislative provision. Second, those countries that have signed the Convention are assessed at least once every five years on the extent to which their legal system and childcare practices conform to the Convention. As you will see in Chapter 6, the United Nations has expressed some concern about the high rate of imprisonment of young offenders in Britain and specifically has drawn attention to the practice of sending 12–14-year-olds into custody (Goldson, 2002).

If you look at the 54 provisions of the Convention, you will see that, apart from the technical provisions concerning jurisdiction and implementation, there are some that seem particularly relevant to social work and the law in the UK. These are as follows.

Table 3.3 United Nations Convention on the Rights of the Child and links to UK law

Article	Focus	Links
2.2	no discrimination on account of what parents do or say	
3	best interests of the child to be a primary consideration for courts and administrative bodies, child protection provision, safety and health	Children Act 1989
5	respect for rights and duties of parents	
6	right to life and development	Human Rights Act 1998
7, 8	right to identity	birth registration provisions
9	separation from parents to be exceptional, proper procedures to apply	
12	child's right to participate in decision-making	Children Act 1989 including placement regulations; Adoption
18	promotion of parental responsibility	Act 1976; Adoption and Children Act 2002
19	protection from abuse or neglect	
21, 22	special status of fostering and adoption	
23	children with disabilities	
24	right to health	health-related legislation
26, 27	right to social security and basic living standards	social security legislation
28, 29	right to education	Education Acts
30	right to own culture	
31	right to play and recreation	
32.9	protection from exploitation, drugs, sexual abuse, abduction, inhuman treatment or punishment, deprivation of liberty without advocacy, participation in armed conflicts	various including criminal law, Human Rights Act 1998, youth justice legislation, Children Act 1989
39	rehabilitation after armed conflict	
40	due legal processes for children accused of committing offences	youth justice legislation especially Powers of Criminal Courts (Sentencing) Act 2000 – see Chapter 6 for further discussion

How are these translated into UK law?

Given that they are not declared as overarching in the same way as the European Convention on Human Rights, this means that in order to answer the question we need to look at specific areas where Parliament has attempted to match UK law to the Convention. Table 3.3 has attempted to do this for you by indicating the areas of legislation or specific

Acts of Parliament that are most relevant – you will also notice that there are some gaps where no specific legislation applies, although there may be other provision through regulations, codes of guidance or policy directives. The Every Child Matters initiative (Department for Education and Skills, 2004) is relevant here for it declares an overall aim that children in the UK should:

- be healthy;

- stay safe;

- enjoy and achieve;

- make a positive contribution;

- achieve economic well-being.

However, when it comes to the actual law itself, the two areas that most directly concern social workers are the Children Act 1989, which specifically facilitates support services for children in need and their parents, and the various provisions relating to education, principally the Education Act 1996. We start with education.

Meeting children's needs for education

CASE STUDY

Declan (aged 16) and his half-sister Clare (aged 4) live with their mother, Trisha, in a house on an estate where the majority of housing is rented from a housing association. The local schools do not have a very enviable reputation. They are low in the league tables of relative achievements in GCSEs and Standard Attainment Tests. Declan's experience of school has been wholly negative and he cannot wait to leave. He has been excluded from school twice in the last year for being abusive to teachers and thinks he was unfairly treated on the last occasion. Trisha is wondering whether there is anything she can do to avoid subjecting Clare to Declan's experience, especially as Clare has a hearing impairment.

The Education Act 1996 consolidates much of the legislation regarding provision of education, but for completeness we also need to look at the Special Educational Needs and Disability Act 2001, which addresses the provision of education for children and students with special needs, and the Education Acts of 2002 and 2005 together with the Education and Inspections Act 2006 which cover matters such as standards, school governance and budgeting. Education is compulsory from the ages of 5 to 16. While children are entitled to start schooling only during the first term after their fifth birthday, in practice many start earlier than this. The Sure Start scheme, introduced by the government in order to address social exclusion and social deprivation through early access to education and related support, has facilitated the inclusion of many 4-year-olds in mainstream education. So it may be possible for Clare to be involved in the school now. Declan, meanwhile, is obliged to wait until the official school leaving date. This will be after his sixteenth birthday – how long after depends on when exactly his birthday occurs.

It is a popular misconception that school attendance is compulsory, whereas in fact it is education that has to be provided by parents. In the vast majority of cases parents will choose to ensure that children receive education by sending them to school, but this is not compulsory. However, if parents choose to have children educated at home (*or otherwise* – section 7 Education Act 1996) they must satisfy the local education authority that this is satisfactory. If school attendance is preferred, parents have the right to express a preference for schooling, but do not have an absolute right of choice. They cannot insist that their children attend a particular school; schools have the right to refuse if they are over-subscribed and their admissions policies, when fairly applied, give priority to other children. So in this case Trisha can decide that local schools are not good enough for Clare, and so send her to another community school in a different area, to a voluntary aided/controlled school or foundation school, or to an independent school. Whichever is chosen the additional costs in terms of fares and/or fees are, of course, the parent's responsibility, although note that Part Six of the Education and Inspections Act 2006 when implemented will extend obligations on local authorities to provide *sustainable modes of travel*.

Responsibility for ensuring that children receive full-time education lies with the local education authority. This duty is carried out primarily through schools checking registers of attendance and reporting to education social workers (education welfare officers), who deal with more than just attendance issues. They are often referred cases where children have special needs, and act as advisers where difficulties at home are having an effect on schooling, or even in some cases where there is abuse. Truancy can result in a parent being prosecuted, or in the child being placed under the supervision of the local education authority where the court, applying the Children Act 1989 principles (see next chapter), is satisfied that the child is not being properly educated. In these cases an education supervision order can be made for up to one year, with possible extensions up to three years (section 36 Children Act 1989).

Education legislation in the UK goes beyond the basics required in the United Nations Convention. Not only is education compulsory, but in state-funded (or partially state-funded) schools, education must be offered in a specific way. There is a national curriculum of core subjects, together with an obligation to provide religious education, although parents have the right to withdraw children from this and from any specifically religious-based assemblies (Education Act 2002), a right which section 55 of the Education and Inspections Act 2006 will extend to sixth-formers. There is also a national code of discipline in the sense that exclusion from school, which is the ultimate penalty, can only be used following the application of certain procedures, and within certain limits (to be further clarified with the implementation of the Education and Inspections Act 2006). Exclusion, unless permanent, can total no more than 45 days in any one school year, and is subject to appeal to the school governing body (Education (Pupil Exclusions and Appeals) (Maintained Schools) (England) Regulations 2002; Education (Pupil Exclusions and Appeals) (Maintained Schools) (Wales) Regulations 2003). The headteacher has the right to exclude (section 52 Education Act 2002), governors can override this and parents have the right to appeal against the governors' decision (Schedule 18 School Standards and Framework Act 1998; School Governance (Procedures) (England) Regulations 2003; Education (School Government) (Wales) Regulations 1999). Note that it is the parents' right to appeal, not the student's, so in the case study it is Trisha who could have appealed, not Declan, a point which seems to run counter to the participation rights enshrined in the United Nations Convention.

The general principle is that all children should be educated in mainstream schooling unless they have special educational needs and their parents wish them to be educated outside the mainstream system (section 1 Special Educational Needs and Disability Act 2001). In this case, Clare would be entitled to an assessment to determine whether she has any learning difficulties arising from her disability (section 312 Education Act 1996). If a statement is issued confirming that she has special needs then the local education authority is under a duty to arrange for those needs to be met. If a statement is refused, parents have the right to appeal to the Special Educational Needs and Disability Tribunal (section 326 Education Act 1996). Note that it is the parent's right to appeal; although Clare is obviously too young to participate, it is worth noting that there is no provision for the child or young person to participate, which likewise appears to be contrary to the principles declared in the United Nations Convention.

Supporting families and helping them to look after children

CASE STUDY

Trisha (whom you met in the previous case study) wants to know what support services are available for her and her family. Declan has no idea what he wants to do when he leaves school, and Trisha is worried that Clare is isolated in their community, with few friends of her own age and with what appears to be an increasingly serious disability.

In this section we examine support services available through a variety of initiatives but primarily through provisions in the Children Act 1989. Before outlining these provisions we need to say something about the values which the Children Act 1989 promotes. Summarising the various sets of guidance and regulations (Department of Health, 1991b) it is possible to discern a number of key principles that underpin the Children Act 1989 and thereby set out the framework for social work with children and families. As we saw in Chapter 1, the Children Act 1989 drew its key concepts and principles from the Cleveland Report (DHSS, 1988), especially in relation to the boundaries between the family, the state and social work agencies, which was why it was important for you to know something of the background to this important piece of legislation. The key principles with regard to supporting families are set out in the official Introduction to the Children Act 1989 (Department of Health, 1989):

- children should usually be brought up in their own family;

- local authorities, working in conjunction with voluntary agencies, should aim to support families offering a range of services appropriate to children's needs;

- services are best delivered by working in partnership with parents;

- parents, and commensurate with their ability to understand, children, should express their wishes and feelings and participate in decision-making.

This is underpinned by some specific requirements in the Children Act 1989 itself. The local authority must *safeguard and promote the welfare of children in their area who are in need* and *promote the upbringing of such children by their families by providing a range and level of services appropriate to those children's needs* (section 17 Children Act 1989). Furthermore the Childcare Act 2006 (Part One England, Part Two Wales) will eventually require local authorities to ensure that there is sufficient child care for parents who are working or are planning to work.

It follows from all of this that court action should be a last resort, in other words only in exceptional circumstances should social workers directly intervene in families to the extent of making decisions that override the parents. For this reason the principles relating to courts and statutory intervention are not addressed here but will feature in Chapter 4. The main emphasis in social work ought to be on providing services to support children and their families. This immediately raises the question of what services, and which children are defined as being 'in need'?

To take the second question first, the answer to this lies in section 17(10) of the Act that offers a list more or less consistent with the United Nations Convention: children who failed to achieve or maintain a reasonable standard of health or development; whose health or development is significantly impaired; or who are disabled. There is a definition of disability in this section and a local authority has a duty to maintain a register of disabled children under Schedule 2(2) of the Act, although both have been subject of some criticism (Braye, 2000; Corker and Davis, 2000). So there is no doubt about it: Clare with her hearing impairment is definitely a child 'in need' and therefore entitled to services arranged through the local authority.

To answer the question about service provision we need to look at Schedule 2 as well as the Children Act 1989 itself. Schedules are mechanisms for providing detail that it would be inappropriate to include in the main body of the Act itself. They are similar to an appendix: important, yet containing material that would interfere with the main substance of a piece of work. Here we find that the Schedules to the Children Act 1989 provide considerable detail as to how the Act itself is to be implemented. It is important to recognise that, as the Schedule is attached to the Act, it does have the force of law. It is not like a Code of Practice which is open to interpretation. Social workers in all sectors of childcare work ought therefore to be familiar with Schedule 2 of the Children Act 1989 as it sets out both additional principles and the mechanisms for achieving the Act's objectives. The Schedule covers a number of different areas and responsibilities. Local authorities are:

- to identify children in need and publish information about services;

- to act to prevent children suffering ill-treatment or neglect;

- at the same time to act to avoid children being involved in court proceedings;

- to take steps to enable children to live with their families and promote contact with them when they are separated from their families;

- to provide family centres, as appropriate, for needs identified by the local authority;

- to provide advice, guidance, counselling, activities, home help, and holidays for children and families where they think this is appropriate.

To this must be added services listed in section 18 of the Children Act 1989 itself:

- day care for children under 5;

- out-of-school and holiday activities.

At the moment we will set aside provision for children outside their own families where parents are unable to continue to look after them, as this is the topic for the next section.

Service provision may include in some exceptional circumstances local authorities offering financial support (section 17(6) Children Act 1989) and for children with disabilities this might include direct payments for services commissioned by the parent (Carers and Disabled Children Act 2000).

Given the range of different services potentially available, it is not surprising that some families find the range confusing and, more importantly, there are sometimes deficiencies. To counteract this, the law provides mechanisms to enhance service co-ordination. Specifically:

- providing information about services offered in the independent sector (Schedule 2);

- a duty to facilitate family support provision by non-statutory organisations (section 17 Children Act 1989);

- a duty to review day-care services in conjunction with education authorities (section 19 Children Act 1989);

- authority to seek help from other authorities in supporting children and families (section 27 Children Act 1989);

- a duty to assist education authorities in providing services for children with special educational needs (section 27 Children Act 1989).

In order to bring this all together local authorities are under a duty to publish Children and Young People's Plans (section 17 Children Act 2004). These plans set out how local authorities propose to meet children's needs in a given area. Co-ordination has become a major issue, given the number of projects and initiatives that now exist to address general and specific needs in children. You may already know what some of these are, but if not, the following exercise will ask you to do some research on this.

ACTIVITY 3.3

Make a list of the initiatives that the government has promoted to enhance the well-being of all children under 16. If you can, find out how these schemes operate in your local area.

The government schemes are listed in the Exercise Answers, pp145–146.

Although this should mean that there will be a number of avenues of support for Trisha and Clare, it will be important for social workers to be aware of how all of these services are integrated (or not as the case may be) and how they relate to legislation and specific policy initiatives. Social workers should note in particular that, before deciding what services to provide, a local authority should ascertain the child's wishes and feelings and give due consideration to them (section 53 Children Act 2004). Also worth noting is the

Childcare Act 2006 which will (when implemented) require early childhood services (early years provision, health services, social services and employment services) to be provided in an integrated manner.

Finally, let's not forget Declan. Although he is 16, he is still entitled to children's services, although it is questionable whether these would be suited to his age group. Rather, the expectation is that he will want to access services for young people (see websites at the end of this chapter for what some of these might be). In England (only) Connexions provides personal advisers assist 13–19-year-olds in matters concerning education, employment, or personal or family life.

Providing substitute care

CASE STUDY

Declan stops attending school and gets involved in a great deal of anti-social behaviour in the local community. Trisha is exasperated with him and is fearful of the bad effect she says he is having on Clare. She decides she does not want him living at home with her any more but has no alternative family members available to help her. In desperation she turns to the local authority and asks them to take him 'into care'.

In responding to Trisha's request, we need to look closely at the Children Act 1989 and note the distinction made between two routes into 'care': being committed to care by courts under a care order (covered in Chapter 4) and responding to a voluntary parental request for 'care'. In fact the term 'in care' is incorrect. The Children Act 1989 introduces the notion of children being *accommodated* or *looked after* rather than being 'in care'. This was deliberate in order to make it very clear that a request by a parent for a local authority to look after a child is like any other request for services, that is, the parent still retains their full parental authority, still keeps all the rights and does not endanger them (as used to be the case under previous legislation) by asking for social work assistance.

Local authorities have a duty to provide accommodation for children in need (see above for explanation of what 'in need' means) where there is no one who has parental responsibility for them, where they are lost or abandoned or, more usually, where the carer is unable to accommodate them (section 20 Children Act 1989). Given the voluntary basis of the request, the local authority cannot accede to it if anyone with parental responsibility can offer care – and this may not necessarily be the parent who is currently looking after the child – or if the child themselves, if they are 16 or over, objects. So in this case Declan would have the right to veto his mother's request, although one wonders what he would suggest as an alternative. In making arrangements for accommodation local authorities must consider the child's wishes and feelings alongside those of people with parental responsibility and others of relevance to the child; give due consideration to religious persuasion, racial origin, cultural and linguistic background; explore potential placements in the child's family and networks; place close to home and with siblings if possible; continue to offer advice and if necessary financial assistance once the child ceases to be looked after (sections 22, 23 and 24 Children Act 1989).

The placement of children in accommodation brings social workers into a whole welter of Regulations which practitioners will need to consult if they are directly involved in placement of children since they are essential guides to practice (a full list appears at the end of this chapter). These primarily concern arrangements for reviews, procedures for checking the suitability of foster carers, appointment of independent visitors (for children who have lost contact with their families of origin), regulations of children's homes and similar matters which are of great importance on a day-to-day basis for the quality of experience of children. Space does not permit a detailed consideration of these here but there is one issue that does need to be addressed, namely the special procedures that apply to children placed in secure accommodation.

Secure accommodation is defined as accommodation provided for the purpose of *restricting liberty* (section 25 Children Act 1989). Local authorities or voluntary organisations may not place the children they look after (those under a care order as well as those who are accommodated) in secure accommodation for more than 72 hours in any 28-day period without reference to a court (regulation 10 Children (Secure Accommodation) Regulations 1991). The purpose of secure accommodation is to deal with those children and young people who have a history of absconding or who are likely to injure themselves unless they can be kept in a restricted environment. A history of absconding has to include a likelihood of suffering significant harm in order to qualify for the provision of such accommodation (section 25 Children Act 1989). There must be an application to court for approval and once the local authority applies to court, an independent guardian will be appointed to look after the interests of the child or young person (for further information on guardians, see the 'Speaking up for children' section in chapter 4). The court will then consider whether the criteria in section 25 are satisfied. If the court agrees to the order, its length should be determined by the welfare needs of the child (Re M (a minor) [1995] FLR 418), and in any case should not exceed three months (regulation 11 Children (Secure Accommodation) Regulations 1991). The order does not require the local authority or voluntary organisation to keep the child in secure accommodation, so is unlike orders that apply to criminal cases, but it grants them the power to do so if they deem it necessary. Do note that these procedures apply even if the child or young person is accommodated by a voluntary request by the parent, although obviously it is open to the parent in such cases to remove the child from local authority accommodation if they see fit.

Providing substitute care also encompasses adoption. This might be regarded as the ultimate request for parents to make of the local authority: to look after their child permanently and to give the child a new home and, in effect, a new identity. It is not proposed to cover adoption law in detail here, but you will find it covered in more comprehensive social work law texts (for example, Brammer, 2007, Chapter 11). Most current law derives from the Adoption and Children Act 2002 which replaced most of the Adoption Act 1976. Requests to place children for adoption are quite specific and fall under separate legislation and rules, for example, governing adoption placement agencies and selection of adopters – foster carers are not considered automatically as potential adopters. Likewise parental agreement can be withdrawn without implying that the parent wishes to withdraw arrangements for accommodation. Consent to an adoption order is a very serious matter and adoptions have to be ratified by a court process, even if full consent is given right the way through. Indeed, proceeding with an adoption order without both parents' full consent is wholly exceptional. UK legislation does allow for the courts to dispense with parental consent on certain grounds (section 52 Adoption and Children Act 2002), but it remains to be seen whether this fully complies with Article 8 of the European Convention on Human Rights concerning rights to family life. As an alternative, courts can now consider special guardianship which does not involve a change of name and is not an order for life, but does provide security in placement (section 115 Adoption and Children Act 2002).

Transition into adulthood

Transition to adulthood is particularly challenging for young people who have been accommodated by the local authority. Substantial research evidence has demonstrated that young people are especially vulnerable to homelessness and generally emerge from local authority accommodation with far fewer educational qualifications and employment prospects than the general population (Bhabra, Ghate and Brazier, 2002). This was recognised by the Children (Leaving Care) Act 2000 which makes amendments to duties under the Children Act 1989. It focuses on the needs of 16- and 17-year-olds who were looked after by local authorities prior to that age – these are designated *eligible children*. The duties towards these eligible children are to provide a personal adviser and to prepare a *pathway plan* for them, which must clearly identify needs and must involve the young person themselves (R (on the application of J) *v* Caerphilly County Borough Council [2005] 2 FCR 153).

There is an obligation to keep in contact with these young people until they attain the age of 21. They are to be offered support and material assistance, which can include financial support. In the case of those continuing to higher or further education, the local authority should offer vacation accommodation (section 4 Children (Leaving Care) Act 2000). The Children Act 2004 (section 9) when implemented will extend the definition of a child to include any 18–20-year-old with learning disabilities who has been 'looked after' by a local authority after the age of 16.

Particular concern has also been expressed by the Social Exclusion Unit about the lack of educational attainment generally by children who have been looked after by local authorities (Social Exclusion Unit, 2003). This concern has resulted in government publications on the education of children in public care, leading on from the Children Act 2004 section 52 requirement to promote the educational achievement of looked after children, together with wider concerns (Department for Education and Skills, 2005; 2006a).

This alerts us to the disadvantage experienced by many young people that is made manifest by the experience of being looked after by local authorities. This raises an important question – and it is for reflection and consideration as it is a philosophical rather than a legal question – does the 'system' prevent children and young people achieving to the same level as the general population and make them particularly vulnerable, or is it that these children and young people have always been particularly vulnerable, having encountered a number of negative life experiences which no system can fully counteract?

What do you think?

C H A P T E R S U M M A R Y

In this chapter, you were challenged to think about definitions of childhood and what ought to constitute children's rights. We then explored ways in which children's basic needs could be met, using as a benchmark the United Nations Convention on the Rights of the Child. In Britain the two important areas that affect children's development are education and social care arrangements to support families. Having summarised what education legislation says about meeting the needs of all children, including those with special needs, we then went on to consider the ways in which social work legislation operates to support families. Here by far the most important legislation is the Children Act 1989, although it is not the only relevant law, and parts of it will be superseded eventually by the Children Act 2004. Some space was given over to an outline of the principles behind this Act as they apply to parents who ask for assistance. We then examined some specifics in terms of the range of services available to children and families, and these were set in the context of other provisions now made by a series of government schemes and initiatives. The last two sections examined the provision of substitute care for children where families cannot look after them, concluding with a consideration of the needs of young people leaving accommodation when they move to adulthood.

In the next chapter, we move on to consider the law as it applies to families when something goes wrong – when they cannot agree about the care of children, or where there are allegations that children are being abused.

FURTHER READING

Department for Education and Skills (2006a) Care Matters Transforming the Lives of Children and Young People in Care. London: Stationery Office.

Department of Health (1991b) Children Act 1989 guidance and regulations. London: HMSO. Volume 1: Court orders. Volume 2: Family support, day care and educational provision for young children. Volume 3: Family placements. Volume 4: Residential care.

Smith, F (2000) Looking After Children: Good Parenting, Good Outcomes. London: Children Act Enterprises.

WEBSITES

4 Nations Child Policy Network: **www.childpolicy.org.uk/**

Careers Wales: **www.careers-gateway.co.uk/cservice/dbpages/10/1007.htm**

Connexions (England): **www.connexions.gov.uk**

Department of Health National Service Framework for Children: **www.dh.gov.uk/en/PolicyAndGuidance/HealthAndSocialCareTopics/ChildrenServices/ChildrenServicesInformation4089111**

Education Otherwise: charity concerned with education of children outside school sytem: **www.education-otherwise.org**

Every Child Matters: **www.everychildmatters.gov.uk/**

Home Office: **www.homeoffice.gov.uk/**

Quality Protects: **www.dfes.gov.uk/qualityprotects/**

Social Exclusion Unit: **www.cabinetoffice.gov.uk/social_exclusion**

Sure Start: **www.surestart.gov.uk/**

United Nations, for Convention on the Rights of the Child in full, adopted by General Assembly resolution 44/25 of 20 November 1989: **www.unhchr.ch/html/menu2/6/crc/treaties/crc.htm**

Welsh Assembly education website: **new.wales.gov.uk/topics/educationandskills/?lang=en**

Chapter 4
Meeting children's needs when things go wrong

Introduction

This chapter is the second of the two-part examination of the law relating to social work with children and families. Leading on from the previous discussion of children's basic needs and rights, and services available to promote their well-being, we now examine the arrangements made to address problems that might occur. The key areas are:

- action that families may take when they cannot agree about arrangements for children;

- what can be done in response to identified needs and shortcomings in meeting those needs;

- how social workers respond to allegations that children are being abused.

Along the way we need to acknowledge what are probably the most disturbing aspects of social work: failure to protect children from death or serious harm, and the abuse of children and young people in placements where they were supposed to be protected and looked after.

As explained in Chapter 3, both these chapters together enable you to attain a number of occupational standards and subject benchmarks. These were clearly set out in the previous chapter and so are not repeated here.

Also outlined in the previous chapter were a number of core principles underpinning social work in this area, many of which are enshrined in the Children Act 1989. To remind you, the basic premise is that children's well-being is best promoted by encouraging and supporting them to live with their own families, and everything should be done to facilitate this. However, there are circumstances in which the advisability of children remaining with their own families becomes questionable, and the law sets out the criteria that need to be fulfilled for social workers or others to intervene directly in families' lives. Before we can consider these, there are two areas that need to be explored. First is the notion of parental responsibility, since it is crucial to understand this in order to be able to operate as a social worker under the Children Act 1989. Second, a number of additional principles come into play when the courts are involved in decision-making regarding children. In Chapter 7 we consider specifically the role of social workers in the court setting, so in this chapter we will be focusing on the powers of intervention in families and the kinds of cases where social workers need to refer cases to court.

Parenthood, parenting and parental responsibility

In this section, we start by drawing a distinction between parenthood, parenting and parental responsibility. The reasons for this will become clear when we discuss the outcome of the next exercise.

ACTIVITY 4.1

How would you distinguish between parenthood, parenting and parental responsibility?

In order to answer this question you may want to think about a number of subsidiary questions:

Is parenthood a legal term?

Who provides parenting? Are biological parents the only people who can offer this?

What are the expectations of parents? What are their responsibilities?

Is there a difference between parental responsibility and parental duties?

This activity should take about 40 minutes, and you may want to join together with others to help answer the questions.

The suggestion that there is a difference between parenthood and parenting is key to understanding law and social work practice in this area.

Parenthood might generally be understood to refer to motherhood and fatherhood, and therefore equated with those people who are the biological mothers and fathers of children. Interestingly, the law does not use the term parenthood, which is a concept rather than a legal status, but does concern itself very much with parental responsibility, which includes defining who might have this. You must not assume that the only people who have parental responsibility are the child's biological parents. This is far from the case. The law is also very clear that there is a difference between *parental duties* and *parental responsibility*. Those who are the child's biological parents clearly have obligations to the child, and the law tends to focus on these obligations as being primarily financial, a duty to *maintain*, enforced, if necessary, by child support legislation – an area not covered in this book. If we take parenting to refer to the process whereby a particular kind of nurturing and development is provided for children, then this kind of 'upbringing' does not necessarily or exclusively have to be provided by biological parents, but naturally if it is provided by someone else, those with parental duties would be expected to pay for it! Parental responsibility covers parental rights in areas such as deciding where a child should live, where they should go to school and how their other welfare needs should be met – protection, discipline, medical treatment, religion, property and so on (White, Carr and Lowe, 2002, Chapter 3). Crucially this also affects status to participate in legal proceedings.

The people who are the child's biological mother and father are automatically people who have parental duties, that is obligations to provide for the child, but may not automatically have parental responsibility, that is all legal rights as parents. However, if the mother and father are married at the time of the child's birth, then they do both share parental responsibility automatically (section 2 Children Act 1989). If they are not married, the mother automatically has parental responsibility, as does the father, if his name is registered on the birth certificate (section 111 Adoption and Children Act 2002). If the father's name was not so registered, it is possible for him to acquire parental responsibility either by marrying, by making a voluntary parental responsibility agreement, or by a court order – a parental responsibility order (section 4 Children Act 1989).

However, parental responsibility is not the exclusive preserve of parents. Other people, such as grandparents or step-parents, might acquire parental responsibility by becoming the child's guardian, or by being granted a residence order or special guardianship order by the court (see below for discussion of residence orders). If children are committed to care under a care order, local authorities also acquire parental responsibility and in this case their right to determine where the child should live overrides that of the parents (section 33 Children Act 1989). Care orders and other court orders are discussed later in this chapter.

Principles that apply to court cases

Before beginning to explore how the law might apply to cases where families are in difficulties, we need to set out underlying principles that govern the way courts decide on disputes brought before them. We have already referred to the promotion of children's upbringing within their own families, but here we need to consider precise guiding principles set out in the Children Act 1989 itself.

First principle

The first principle is that when courts consider cases, the child's welfare is paramount (section 1 (1) Children Act 1989). This also applies to adoption cases by virtue of section 1 (2) Adoption and Children Act 2002. Note that this principle governs court considerations and does not apply to everything the local authority or parents might do to promote the welfare of children in terms of providing support, nor does it mean that it is the only consideration or that it always applies (White, Carr and Lowe, 2002; Brammer, 2007, pp183, 334). Without going into too much detail about this, suffice it to say that this means, for example, that courts would not ignore concerns for public safety if anti-social behaviour issues were at stake and other legislation such as the Crime and Disorder Act 1998 applied. In a similar way the courts in adoption cases might take a very long-term view which apparently ignored the immediate short-term welfare interests of the child.

Second principle

The second principle is that delay in hearing cases is deemed prejudicial to children's welfare. This is fairly self-explanatory but clearly is of great concern when the courts themselves have a backlog of cases, or where there is a shortage of staff able to deal with them. Note that this does not mean that cases must be heard hastily or without proper assessment. Given the first principle it will always be the case that courts will give full consideration to the case and expect a comprehensive analysis of the child's needs and alternative courses of action. Similarly, case law (for example Re B (a minor) [1994] 2 FLR 269) suggests courts will allow time to see if particular courses of action might be beneficial.

Third principle

The third principle is that in deciding disputed cases, courts should pay particular regard to the welfare checklist, namely:

- the ascertainable wishes and feelings of the child;

- physical, emotional and educational needs;

- likely effects of changing circumstances;

- age, sex, background and any other relevant characteristics;

- potential or actual harm;

- the capabilities of parents and others in meeting the child's needs;

- the range of powers available to the court.

There is clearly a major social work practice issue concerning how one determines the wishes and feelings of very young children. Ascertaining children's views is a key role of children's guardians appointed in public law proceedings (see later in this chapter and Chapter 7). The list in the Children Act 1989 is often used by professionals as a reminder of the various aspects of children's welfare they need to take into consideration. It is a key element in the Department of Health guidance on assessment (Department of Health, 2000c). It is not proposed to go through each aspect of the welfare checklist here but they must be borne in mind when considering intervention in families, and social workers must consider the checklist most especially in cases involving allegations of abuse. It is self-evident that the list would be relevant where there are disputes between parents about arrangements for children. It may be worth noting, nevertheless, that in terms of background, attention must be paid to race, culture and religion. There are a number of cases in this area which are summarised in the standard social work law texts (Ball and McDonald, 2002; Brammer, 2007; Brayne and Carr, 2005; Vernon, 2005) and if you are practising in this area you will need to know what these are.

Fourth principle

The fourth principle is what some refer to as the *no order* principle, that is to say that generally speaking courts should avoid making any order at all unless it is considered that making an order is better for the child than not making one. There is much misunderstanding about this, with a belief in some quarters that this is some kind of legal presumption against making orders even where children have been demonstrated to be subjected to harm. This is not the case. It might be more accurate to say that this is a *no unnecessary order principle* (White, Carr and Lowe, 2002, p47). Two specific issues are relevant to social work practice. One is that social workers often assume that this means that if people can be persuaded to agree during court proceedings the court need not then make any kind of order. There may still be overriding reasons for rejecting this, for example if making a residence order is necessary in order to give a person looking after the child parental responsibility (as in the case of re G (children) [2005] EWCA Civ 1283). The second issue is that where actions currently already comply with the likely court order, for example contact already takes place, courts are unlikely to see the need to make an order. In fact an order would secure existing arrangements and might also be what the child wants. The Children and Adoption Act 2006 extends this principle by enabling courts to make directions that facilitate contact without actually making a contact order.

Disputes within families

> **CASE STUDY**
>
> *Suzanne and Winston are unable to agree about who should look after their three children now that they have split up. Samuel (14) wants to go with his father. Jasmine (9) and Rebecca (6) want to stay with their mother. Suzanne wants all three children with her, arguing that she needs Samuel to look after the two girls. Winston wants all three children, arguing that by 'walking out' on the family, Suzanne has forfeited her right to look after any of them.*

Cases such as this are regarded as 'private' law cases, since the dispute is within the family, not between the family and the local authority. All of the relevant orders will be found in section 8 Children Act 1989, and these comprise four kinds:

● residence orders which concern where children will live;

● contact orders which concern arrangements for children to keep in touch with others;

● prohibited steps orders which stop someone doing something;

● specific issue orders which compel someone to do something.

The orders are not exclusive to disputes within families; in some cases they may be appropriate in care proceedings as an alternative to care orders or supervision orders.

So in this particular case study, mother and father would, if they cannot resolve their dispute, be applying for residence orders. Note that if the parents are not married, Winston still has a legal right to make the application (Re C (minors) (parent: residence order) [1993] 3 All ER 313 CA). The fourth principle set out above should impel parents and their solicitors to try to reach some kind of agreement if at all possible. Nevertheless if it is irresolvable the courts will have to make some kind of decision. Clearly in this case courts will be very exercised by what is in the overall interests of each child, and the third principle would direct them to be strongly influenced by the children's own individual wishes and feelings. Court practice would invariably follow the social work principle of according greater weight to older children's wishes and so it is very likely that Samuel's wishes would prevail over Suzanne's desire to have someone looking after her daughters. The court would certainly not be impressed by a desire to 'punish' one parent by denying them a residence order. Once courts have decided about where children should live, the assumption is that there would then be an agreement about when the other parent could have contact with the child. It is not automatic that courts will make contact orders as well as residence orders, but may do so if there is, again, failure to agree. As an alternative, courts might grant joint residence orders, where parents share decision-making more equitably, sometimes even if the parents' relationship is not totally harmonious (re R (residence: shared care: children's views) [2005] EWCA Civ 542).

It may be worth saying something about the effect of residence orders. These do not divest the other parent of their parental rights and duties, but they do give the person with the residence order the right to say where the child will live and make day-to-day decisions about them. If a father, not married to the mother and not otherwise entitled to parental responsibility, is awarded a residence order, he is automatically awarded a separate parental responsibility order (section 12 Children Act 1989). Residence orders do not allow for a change of the child's name or identity, nor do they permit someone to take a child abroad, except for a holiday up to a month.

It is not only parents who can apply for residence orders. So can others who have an interest in the child, but in this case only with the permission of the court although the Adoption and Children Act 2002 (section 112) strengthens the position of step-parents in this regard. This may be very useful in cases where, for example, grandparents end up caring for a child on a long-term basis. Indeed, in such cases a residence order is quite advisable as it secures the long-term future of the child and clarifies the grandparents' legal rights and responsibilities. An application for a residence order is also one way of discharging a care order, but we will come to this point later.

Contact orders in effect compel someone to allow a child to communicate with, or even to stay temporarily with, someone else – for example, to go on holiday with the other parent. In effect the court is ordering the person looking after the child to allow contact, and they must do so or risk some kind of penalty such as imprisonment (re M (contact order) [2005] EWCA Civ 615) or, in future, an unpaid work requirement or compensation (Children and Adoption Act 2006). There have been a number of particularly contentious cases where courts have made contact orders even where there has been a record of violence (in A v N (Refusal of Contact) [1997] 1 FLR 533 the court imprisoned a mother for six weeks for obstructing contact in these circumstances). Here the courts are persuaded by what is in the interests of the child, namely that they should continue to see both parents, rather than using contact orders as a way of penalising parents who have been abusive. However, in serious cases courts may stop contact altogether, although not just because they are engaged in permanency planning for children (re H (termination of contact) [2005] EWCA Civ 318).

A prohibited steps order is precisely what it says: it stops someone from doing something. In addition to denying an adult contact with the child, these orders have been used to prevent a change of school, a change in religion, a change of name and particular procedures such as circumcision where not medically justifiable (re S (specific issue order: religion: circumcision) [2004] EWHC 1282). The converse to these orders are specific issue orders which have been made in cases where, for example, it is necessary to override refusal to agree to a blood transfusion, to order that children should attend a particular school, and in the most contentious case of all, to compel a 17-year-old with a severe learning disability to be sterilised (Re HG (specific issue: sterilisation) [1993] 1 FLR 587). These orders cannot be used as backdoor 'ouster' orders, that is, as ways of compelling someone to leave the home. Nor can they be used as a way of achieving the same ends as residence and contact orders.

These kinds of orders should not generally be made in relation to young people of the age of 16 or above (section 9 Children Act 1989) although section 114 Adoption and Children Act 2002 gives the courts discretion to extend the order to age 18. Apart from a residence order, the courts cannot make these kinds of orders in relation to children who are subject to care orders. In addition to, or as an alternative to, these orders, courts may decide that it would be appropriate to offer advice or assistance through CAFCASS (Children and Family Court Advisory and Support Service) or the local authority, in which case it is open to them to make a Family Assistance Order (section 16 Children Act 1989). This is a short-term order, up to six months, and is intended to try to resolve these issues without needing to make private law court orders.

Child protection investigations

ACTIVITY *4.2*

Look at the following brief scenarios and say whether you think in each case they are examples of abuse or not. Do not sit on the fence! You should try to make a definite yes or no decision. If you decide that they are examples of abuse, what kind of abuse would it be: physical, emotional, sexual or neglect? Obviously in reality you would have far more information, but the point of this exercise is to get you thinking about definitions of abuse. You might like to try this exercise in a small group in which case be prepared for a wide variety of opinion on some of the scenarios!

1. *Children aged 5 and 3 who are left on their own for three or four hours every Friday evening.*

2. *A girl of 10 who is expected to spend an hour on household chores in the morning before going to school.*

3. *Children under 5 who have been punished by being shut in a cupboard for half-an-hour.*

4. *A 9-month-old child who has bite marks on her arm.*

5. *A 3-year-old who engages in highly sexualised play with his 14-year-old uncle.*

6. *Two boys of 5 and 8 who are beaten by their father with a leather belt.*

Having completed the exercise, you will no doubt have realised that part of its purpose is to demonstrate that deciding what constitutes abuse is not always easy. You will find commentary on the questions in the Exercise Answers, pp146–147.

The exercise and commentary on the scenarios use the four official categories under which children can be formally registered as being at risk of abuse. Two important sets of procedures and guidance relevant here are: *Working together to safeguard children* (HM Government, 2006) and *Framework for the assessment of children in need and their families* (Department of Health, 2000c). These set out the ways in which local authorities and other agencies need to set about protecting children. By 2008 the key responsibility for implementing the child protection system will be transferred from social services departments to Directorates of Children's Services (section 18 Children Act 2004). We have already seen that local authorities have a duty to promote the welfare of children 'in need', but in addition there is a specific responsibility for making inquiries in collaboration with other authorities in cases of alleged harm to a child (section 47 Children Act 1989). Specifically the local authority must:

- consider whether it is necessary to apply to court for an order, especially if refused access to the child;

- see the child unless they already have sufficient information to make a decision;

- if they decide not to apply for an order, consider whether and when to review the case.

Furthermore, the local authority can be obliged by a court to instigate an investigation where a court is hearing a family proceedings case (broadly the kind of cases we are considering in this chapter) and it appears to the court that a care or supervision order might be appropriate. The local authority must consider whether it should apply for a care or supervision order, whether it should provide services, or take some other action. The local authority must, however, report to the court if it decides not to seek a care or supervision order, giving reasons and indicating other action taken or proposed (section 37 Children Act 1989).

All of this underlines the importance of the assessment process and the way in which investigations of alleged abuse are undertaken, taking all relevant factors into consideration. Assessment is an absolutely critical area of social work practice (see Parker and Bradley, 2007). In this book we focus on how the law guides the assessment process, examining the various stages and highlighting the legal criteria that govern procedures.

So, first of all, what are we actually assessing, from the law's perspective? The short answer to this is *significant harm*. Is there evidence of a child possibly currently suffering significant harm? Is there evidence of the possibility of a child likely to be suffering significant harm? The concept of significant harm is very important and was deliberately introduced into the Children Act 1989 (section 31) following on from the Cleveland Report's recommendations (DHSS, 1988). It is not sufficient to prove just that a child suffered some kind of harm: the harm has to be of a degree that indicates some impediment to the child's health, development or welfare. Ill-treatment would obviously include sexual abuse but might also encompass emotional abuse if this were deliberate. Health includes all those needs that we identified at the start of this chapter: physical, emotional, social, educational and so on. The next section explores this in more detail as this is such a critical area, determining the extent to which the law authorises intervention in families, but for now we need simply to bear in mind that the assessment should be considering whether there is a possibility of significant harm, the extent of it and presenting a preliminary analysis of some of its causes. The outcomes of the assessment and the conclusions ultimately drawn from it might eventually need to be considered by the court under care proceedings.

The supervisory body for implementing child protection procedures in each area is the Local Safeguarding Children Board. This is an inter-agency body charged with co-ordinating child protection work and establishing procedures for agencies to follow, with appropriate representation to guarantee this (sections 13 and 14 Children Act 2004; for England The Local Safeguarding Children Boards Regulations 2006; for Wales The Local Safeguarding Children Boards (Wales) Regulations 2006). At the local level, individual cases are dealt with by Child Protection Conferences, which bring professionals and family together following an initial assessment as to whether there is cause for concern in a particular case (a section 47 inquiry, as it is often termed). The Child Protection Conference has to:

- co-ordinate information;

- decide whether a child has been harmed or is likely to suffer harm;

- decide what action to take, including whether to register the child, and what inter-agency child protection plan needs to be drawn up.

Registering the child means putting the name of the child on the official Child Protection register. This is not like making a court decision, it is simply a device for ensuring that various agencies know about a child who has possibly suffered, or is at risk of suffering, harm. It is therefore a working document and case law (for example R *v* Hampshire County Council, *ex parte* H [1999] 2 FLR 359) has confirmed that courts will rarely intervene in decisions to place children's names on the register, but there must be some evidence to justify this action – one or more identifiable incidents that have adversely affected the child. Access to the register must be carefully controlled and obviously is confidential.

One issue possibly unique to child protection is the extent of joint investigation between the police and social workers. Not surprisingly, where there are allegations of abuse concerning a child there are often allegations concerning who has caused the abuse. This means that the police may wish to conduct a criminal investigation. Home Office and Department of Health guidance points out that to obtain the best evidence in criminal proceedings the child should be interviewed jointly by a police officer and social worker, and this will be particularly important in cases of allegations of sexual abuse (Home Office, 2002a). Not only will this be a joint interview, but good practice suggests that it should be video recorded. In criminal trials there is then the potential for the video to be used to avoid the necessity of the child appearing in court in person. In care proceedings cases the video could potentially be used, and case law confirms that in some instances ought to be used (B *v* Torbay Council [2006] Fam Law 924; Re M (a child) (care proceedings: witness summons) [2007] EWCA Civ 9), but remember that the burden of proof in care proceedings, which are civil cases, is not as stringent as that required in criminal cases (see Chapter 1, Table 1.1).

As to what happens after the investigation, there is a set procedure, summarised diagrammatically in *Working together* (HM Government, 2006: pp142–146) and presented in an amended form on the next page. From this it will be seen that much depends on decisions at various stages: not just child protection conferences, but also various strategy meetings held within the children's services authority.

Working together diagram

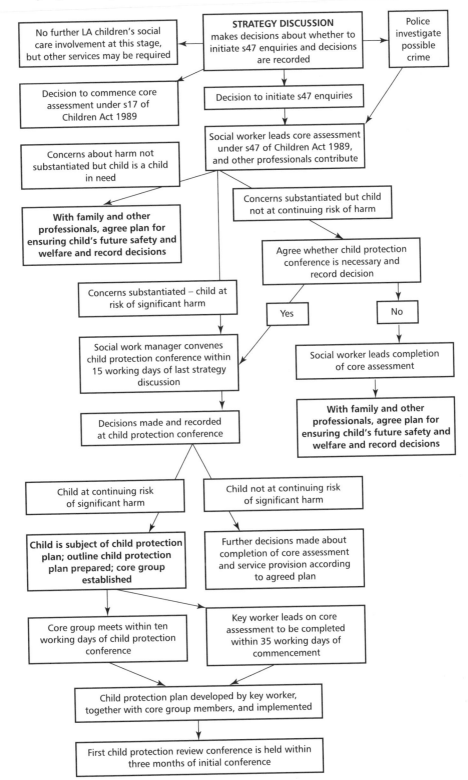

What if people do not co-operate with the child protection investigation or assessment? One possibility then is a child assessment order. Its purpose is simply to allow an assessment of the child's needs, despite parental objections. It is not intended as an emergency order. It must be obtained by making application to a court, who may appoint a guardian to represent the child's interests (section 41 Children Act 1989). The grounds for the order set out in section 43 Children Act 1989 are:

- there is reasonable cause to suspect that the child is suffering or is likely to suffer significant harm;

- an assessment of the child's health or development is required to determine this;

- assessment is unlikely without an order.

A child assessment order, if granted, directs any person who can to produce the child to the person named in the order, imposes duties to comply with court directions, authorises assessment, subject to the child's consent. The order may not last more than seven days (section 43 Children Act 1989). A child assessment order is inappropriate if it is necessary to protect the child by removing them – a Child Assessment Order does not convey this authority and here an emergency protection order would be more appropriate. This probably explains why in practice child assessment orders are quite rare (White, Carr and Lowe, 2002, p238).

If it is necessary to remove children from home in order to assess whether they need protection, this moves us into the area of direct intervention, which in turn raises fundamental questions about the rights of social workers and other agencies to separate children from their parents.

Child protection intervention

CASE STUDY

Megan aged 5 and Michael aged 3 are once again left on their own this Friday evening. The police are called by neighbours and they in turn contact the local authority children's services (children's social care). By midnight no adult has returned to the home.

You may well consider that in this situation the children should be taken to a safe place for the night – although this may not be the only alternative. If the police are to take action, this should only be considered as a very short-term measure, necessary in order to provide immediate safety and in order for the children's service authority to start an investigation.

The immediate challenge of the case, however, is for the police or the social worker to gain access to the children.

The social worker may only enter or search premises with the permission of the owner or occupier, with the authority of an emergency protection order and then only if stipulated (section 48(3) Children Act 1989), with a warrant issued under specific provisions in the Children Act 1989 and then only when accompanied by a police officer, or under the authority of a recovery order issued where children go missing from care or a place of safety (section 50 Children Act 1989). The same provisions apply to the police, except that, in addition, the police may enter premises without a warrant to save or preserve life in a *life or limb* situation (section 17(1)(e) Police and Criminal Evidence Act 1984).

Having gained access to the home, what then should happen?

The police have powers to protect children without reference to the court. The grounds are that there is reasonable cause to believe that the child would otherwise be likely to suffer significant harm (section 46 Children Act 1989). By removing the child under these powers, the police are to make arrangements for accommodation, detain children there and prevent their removal, and must appoint a designated officer to safeguard the welfare of the child. The police then have a duty to inform the local authority of the case, and must allow reasonable contact by relatives. The police child protection order lasts for an initial period of up to 72 hours and cannot be renewed. The next stage is for the police or local authority to apply to the court for an emergency protection order unless the order is allowed to lapse (section 46 Children Act 1989), although there are some circumstances in which police powers can be used even though an emergency protection order is in force (Langley v Liverpool City Council [2005] EWCA Civ 1173).

Social workers do not have powers to protect children without reference to the court or to a magistrate. Any person (yes, literally any person) can apply for an emergency protection order for a child but only the local authority or the National Society for the Prevention of Cruelty to Children (NSPCC) can subsequently bring care proceedings. Applications can be made either *by summons*, that is, through the court having told people that you are intending to do this, or *ex parte*, that is direct to a single magistrate in the absence of anyone else – in which case the decision can be challenged in court within 72 hours (section 45 Children Act 1989). The purpose of an emergency protection order is to permit removal of a child in an emergency, to prevent the removal of a child from accommodation or hospital, or to enable essential medical treatment to be authorised in an emergency. The grounds stipulated in section 44 Children Act 1989 are:

- there is reasonable cause to believe that the child is likely to suffer significant harm unless removed or detained;

- enquiries are being made by the local authority under section 47 as to whether the child is suffering, or is likely to suffer significant harm;

- the local authority has reasonable cause to suspect significant harm and its investigation is being frustrated by unreasonable refusal of access to the child;

- the applicant has reasonable cause to believe that access is required as a matter of urgency.

The court has the power to appoint a guardian when it makes an emergency protection order unless it is satisfied that it is not necessary to do so (section 41 Children Act 1989).

The effect of an emergency protection order under section 44 Children Act 1989 is that it:

- directs any person who can to produce the child;

- authorises removal of the child where this is necessary for welfare;

- prevents removal of the child where this is necessary for welfare;

- for the duration of the order gives the applicant parental responsibility but only allows action which is reasonably required for the child's welfare, e.g. consent to urgent medical treatment (note this does not divest anyone of parental responsibility);

- may, if endorsed to this effect, authorise entry and search of premises;

- can limit or prevent contact with the child if the court so directs: the court must consider contact arrangements;

- can authorise assessment: the court should give directions about this.

It is also possible to include exclusion orders so that people who pose a risk to the child can be ordered to leave temporarily (section 44A Children Act 1989 inserted by Family Law Act 1996). The emergency protection order initially lasts up to eight days, and can be extended once for seven days, but the principle is only to grant the order until the first available date for consideration of an interim order or some other action (section 45 Children Act 1989).

So in this case study there are various possibilities, and which is pursued will probably depend on local arrangements, but it is quite likely that the case will be referred to court fairly swiftly for some kind of decision as to what should happen next.

Let us suppose that the police take action to protect the children, the local authority applies for, and is granted, an emergency protection order. What happens next to Megan and Michael?

By this time a guardian should have been appointed to look after their interests and ascertain their wishes and feelings. Clearly a fair amount of work would have to be done in terms of finding out a great deal more about the family and the circumstances that led to the children being neglected. However, in order to think about what happens next, we need to think more widely about the overall plan for both children. It is tempting, far too tempting, to think in terms of punishing parents for allowing children to be exposed to potential harm and for considering family proceedings orders as being somehow proportionate to the degree of harm to which children have been exposed. Such thinking is, however, utterly wrong. Once the immediate situation has been addressed, social workers must consider very carefully what is in the best long-term interests of the children.

The preliminary consideration when intervening directly in families, especially when removing children from their parents' care, is the overall purpose of intervention. In cases of extreme abuse it may be obvious that the child needs some kind of sanctuary, but if this is the care system, how long should the child remain there? It is not axiomatic that the child should be taken into care and kept there for a lengthy period simply because the abuse was apparently severe. In the case of Megan and Michael, supposing that they were taken into care for a short period, at what point could they be returned to the parents? When the parents or parent understood how dangerous it was to leave children this young? When the parents changed their lifestyle? After they had attended parenting classes? These are all valid professional social work questions, and clearly much depends on the individual circumstances of the case and assessment of the parents' capabilities.

This kind of thinking lies behind the Children Act 1989, for it envisages emergency protection orders, interim care orders and care orders as being very much a last resort. Furthermore, even if a care order is made, parents do not lose their right to participate in children's lives. A care order is an order that transfers some parental responsibilities and rights, especially concerning where the child should live, to the local authority. It does not 'write off' the parents, and it certainly does not mean the child has to remain physically in care until they are 18, although that is when care orders formally end unless revoked earlier. There are provisions for children being returned to their families even whilst the care order continues to be in force (section 23 Children Act 1989 and Placement of Children with Parents Regulations 1991). Care orders can be discharged by the court, and parents and children themselves, if they are old enough to understand and give instructions to solicitors, can apply (section 39 Children Act 1989) and there need to be strong grounds for resisting this revocation application.

Furthermore, there are alternatives to care orders. The court might consider making a supervision order, or might consider agreeing to the child living with another relative under a residence order. The Children Act 1989 encourages courts and social workers to view statutory care as a last resort, although it should never be forgotten that for some children it is this last resort that has literally saved their lives. Unfortunately, however, even within the care system, there have been cases of children being abused (see next section) so we should never assume that a care order is always the best option.

So let us suppose that in this case study the parents are not co-operative and the local authority reluctantly concludes that they must take some action. Whilst the case is being investigated and assessments are being formulated, the case will need to be adjourned for a few weeks. But if the children are in care, probably with foster carers, the court cannot just adjourn the case but must consider what interim measures to put in place. After an emergency protection order, the most likely step to be considered is an interim care order, or even a series of interim orders for there can be as many of them as are necessary before the case is fully heard. The criteria for interim orders differ from the grounds for an emergency protection order since now the court must decide that they have reasonable grounds for believing that there are grounds for the full care order (section 38 Children Act 1989). Nevertheless there is no expectation that just because the court grants an interim care order, it will eventually grant a full care order. In any case there is a difference between declaring *reasonable grounds for believing* and concluding that the grounds for a care order are *satisfied*.

The grounds for a full care order are the same as for those for making any order under care proceedings, namely there must be proof that the child is suffering *significant harm*. To be precise the court has to be convinced that the child concerned is suffering, or is likely to suffer, significant harm and that harm can be attributed to the child being beyond parental control, or it can be attributed to the fact that the care which the child is receiving or is likely to receive differs from what it would be reasonable to expect parents to offer (section 31(2) Children Act 1989). Having adjudicated on this threshold criteria, the court would then consider what kind of order would best meet the child's needs.

This all sounds very complicated so let us take it stage by stage. Case law has established that in cases of alleged harm courts should consider two issues separately (Humberside County Council *v* B [1993] 1 FLR 257). First, it has to decide factually whether the child is being harmed or is in a situation where they are likely to be harmed unless the court takes some action. Harm is ill-treatment, which obviously includes sexual abuse, but may also extend to emotional abuse, or impairment of health or development. Health may include mental health, and development refers to all aspects of development (as discussed earlier in this chapter); the Adoption and Children Act 2002 (section 120) extends this to include *seeing or hearing the ill-treatment of another*. To assess impairment of health or development the law says practitioners need to compare this child with what could reasonably be expected of a similar child. If the harm arises from the child's being beyond parental control, then the threshold criteria are met. Otherwise the harm has to derive from parents failing to offer the level or quality of care which it would be reasonable to expect. A diagram, adapted from White, Carr and Lowe (2002, p263) may simplify this.

Significant harm threshold criteria

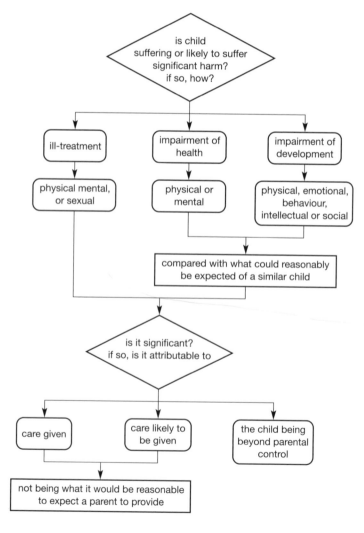

In our case study it would be reasonable to expect parents to look after a 5- and a 3-year-old directly themselves, or else to provide someone to carry out this task for them. To leave children of this age unattended and uncared for during the night would be, most people would agree, unreasonable. And harm, in terms of potential physical harm is obvious, as is the actual emotional harm caused by fear and anxiety. So in this case the threshold criteria might well be proven. Next, the court considers what to do about it, and here they look at the needs of the children and their welfare, and specifically the welfare checklist contained in section 1 of the Children Act 1989. At this second stage the court considers whether or not to make an order, even though the harm is proven: remember the *no unnecessary order* principle? If it decides to make an order, the court then considers what kind of order to make. Is there a grandparent who can offer the children a home? If so, and they are willing and suitable to care for the children, why not make a residence order in their favour? If there are no other alternatives, the court will need to consider supervision orders or care orders.

A supervision order gives the supervisor the duty to *advise, assist and befriend* the child (section 35 Children Act 1989). The child remains living at home, but the order might require the child to submit to some kind of medical examination, subject to the child's informed consent. There can be a requirement to participate in certain activities, and clearly there is an expectation that there would be regular visits, although there are no regulations about this. The supervision order lasts initially for up to one year, but can be extended for up to three years if the supervisor applies for this (Schedule 3 Children Act 1989).

Before making a care order, courts must consider two important issues. First is Article 8 of the European Convention on Human Rights (see Chapter 2), which implies that care orders should be regarded as temporary measures, and that the order must be proportionate and necessary (White Carr and Lowe, 2002, p284). Therefore the local authority should consider alternative family placements, and might even consider placing the child at home under the aegis of the care order, since the care order still gives the authority the right to remove the child if need be. Critically, the court must consider the local authority's intentions for the child once they are awarded the care order. This is the care plan, and the plan must be *viable* (re R (care: plan for adoption: best interest) [2006] 1 FLR 483). The extent of courts' control and supervision of care plans is contentious following a House of Lords decision overruling an attempt to introduce a *starring system* whereby the courts could review the implementation of care plans once care orders were made (re S (Minors) (care order: implementation of care plan) [2002] LGR 251). The Appeal Court had concluded they could do this because of their interpretation of the European Convention on Human Rights, but the position now is that once care orders are made, courts will not review them unless someone makes an application for a variation in contact or a discharge of the care order. The Adoption and Children Act 2002 (section 121) obliges the court to consider the care plan before making a care order.

Care orders have the effect of discharging any section 8 order. Once made, care orders can be discharged by application to the court by the local authority, the child or anyone who has parental responsibility (section 39 Children Act 1989). It is possible to appeal against the making of a care order.

The second issue the court must consider before making care orders are the arrangements for contact between the child and people of significance to the child. There is a presumption in favour of contact between the child and family members, so any restriction on contact must have a court order (section 34 Children Act 1989). If there is someone who poses a potential danger to the child, it is possible to order that contact be supervised, and also contact can be defined or even prohibited. If necessary the local authority can make emergency arrangements to refuse contact for up to seven days where they believe this is consistent with the promotion of the child's welfare (section 34 Children Act 1989). Once the court hears the case it may make any order it sees fit in relation to contact, and impose appropriate conditions, providing it is convinced that this is consistent with the promotion of the welfare of the child. Note that these are not the same as section 8 contact orders, made in private law cases. Naturally the child's wishes and feelings will be considered, usually interpreted to the court through the guardian although sometimes articulated on their behalf by a lawyer.

This appropriately brings us on to the issue of speaking on behalf of children and acting as their advocates.

Speaking up for children

Generally speaking children do not participate in court proceedings (Chapter 7 addresses court work in greater detail). They are, however, a party to the proceedings, that is, they have the right to address the court through a lawyer, and additionally children have a guardian allocated to them who will ascertain their wishes and feelings and present them to the court through a comprehensive report and oral evidence. Children's guardians are appointed by CAFCASS (section 12 Criminal Justice and Court Services Act 2000). Guardians may compile reports for the court in private law family proceedings, but the bulk of their work is carried out in public law care proceedings where they furnish comprehensive reports to the court and also give evidence if required. They must be appointed where courts are considering a care or supervision order, section 37 directions (obliging local authorities to assess harm in private law cases), discharge of care orders or variation and discharge of supervision orders, contact orders under care orders (note not section 8 contact orders) and in some other proceedings (section 41 Children Act 1989).

In the next chapter we devote a section to user perspectives and experiences of the courts and advocacy, but suffice it to say here that the overall message from parents and children is a desire to take a greater part in the decision-making process. Lack of full consultation is a recurrent theme (Thoburn, Lewis and Shemmings, 1995). For a complete summary of relevant research into the operation of the Children Act 1989, it is well worth consulting *Messages from Research* (Aldgate, 2001) and the periodic Children Act Reports (Department for Education and Skills, 2006b).

System failure

What happens when the system appears to fail? At the first level, there are of course complaints procedures. In relation to the Children Act 1989, these are more formalised and run alongside the system for conducting regular reviews of cases (section 26 Children Act 1989). There is then the potential to apply to the local government ombudsman if there is an allegation of maladministration. Alternatively or in addition, it is open for service users to apply to the courts under common law for judicial review of local authority decisions. One example of this concerned the decision by a local authority to consider someone as posing a risk to children even though he had been acquitted on sexual abuse charges. This was held to be lawful as section 47 of the Children Act 1989 concerned reasonable cause to suspect abuse, not a definite conclusion that there had been (R (on the application of S) *v* Swindon Borough Council [2001] 2 FLR 776). Concerning a local authority's apparent failure to act, there are the Secretary of State's default powers, powers of inspection and power to hold inquiries (sections 84, 80 and 81 Children Act 1989 respectively; Inquiries Act 2005). Inquiries are most often held where a child has been killed or seriously harmed, and where it is considered action could have been taken to prevent this, but they may also be appropriate where children have been abused within the care system itself.

No summary of child protection social work would be complete without reference, regrettably, to cases where things have gone badly wrong. In the 1980s and 1990s there were a substantial number of inquiries where children had been killed or seriously injured, and it is not proposed to summarise all of these. Instead, we shall look at two fundamental areas: child protection supervision failures, as demonstrated in the recent Victoria Climbié case, and institutional abuse that occurred in Staffordshire and North Wales.

CASE STUDY

The Victoria Climbié Case

At the post-mortem examination, Dr Carey recorded evidence of no fewer than 128 separate injuries to Victoria's body, saying, There really is not anywhere that is spared – there is scarring all over the body. Therefore, in the space of just a few months, Victoria had been transformed from a healthy, lively, and happy little girl, into a wretched and broken wreck of a human being. Perhaps the most painful of all the distressing events of Victoria's short life in this country is that even towards the end, she might have been saved. In the last few weeks before she died, a social worker called at her home several times. She got no reply when she knocked at the door and assumed that Victoria and Kouao had moved away. It is possible that at the time, Victoria was in fact lying just a few yards away, in the prison of the bath, desperately hoping someone might find her and come to her rescue before her life ebbed away.
(Department of Health and Home Office, 2003, 1.9–1.11)

So what went wrong? To answer that in terms of poor professional practice you need to read the Victoria Climbié Inquiry Report in detail since this catalogues the failures on the part of social work, police and medical staff who should have acted to prevent the continuous persistent abuse. It is harrowing reading, but important lessons need to be drawn from it. The Inquiry Report does just this, setting out 108 recommendations for change. Lord Laming pledged that Victoria's suffering would mark an *enduring turning point in ensuring proper protection of children in this country*. The inquiry was extensive, costing £3.8 million and hearing from 158 witnesses and 121 child protection experts. The report concluded that the child protection system failed as a result of a lamentable lack of *basic good practice* by front-line staff and, especially, senior managers failing to take responsibility for the failings of their organisations. Some recommendations applied to direct practice, so may be worth highlighting; in particular:

CASE STUDY

Recommendation 34

Social workers must not undertake home visits without being clear about the purpose of the visit, the information to be gathered during the course of it, and the steps to be taken if no one is at home...

Recommendation 35

Directors of social services must ensure that children who are the subject of allegations of deliberate harm are seen and spoken to within 24 hours of the allegation being communicated to social services...

Recommendation 36

No emergency action on a case concerning an allegation of deliberate harm to a child should be taken without first obtaining legal advice...

Recommendation 45

Directors of social services must ensure that the work of staff working directly with children is regularly supervised. This must include the supervisor reading, reviewing and signing the case file at regular intervals.

Recommendation 51

Directors of social services must ensure that all strategy meetings and discussions involve the following three basic steps:

- *a list of action points must be drawn up, each with an agreed timescale and the identity of the person responsible for carrying it out;*

- *a clear record of the discussion or meeting must be circulated to all those present and all those with responsibility for an action point;*

- *a mechanism for reviewing completion of the agreed actions must be specified. The date upon which the first such review is to take place is to be agreed and documented.*

The government's response was to issue a Green Paper outlining proposed changes to the organisation of services which culminated in the Children Act 2004, along with a number of publications under the heading 'Every Child Matters' (see list at the end of this chapter). At the same time, overall responsibility for childcare social work services provided by local authorities was transferred from the Department of Health to the Department for Education and Skills. In 2005 the first Children's Commissioner for England was appointed, the first Children's Commissioner (for Wales) having been appointed in 2001 under the Children's Commissioner for Wales Act 2001. The Commissioners' main role is to champion the interests of children, compile reports and conduct general investigations. At the same time in both England and Wales, local authorities subsequently began the task of integrating children's services and appointing the first Directors and lead members of Children's Services as required by sections 18 and 19 of the Children Act 2004.

Other examples of inquiries of which practitioners ought to be aware include inappropriate restraint of young people in residential care in Staffordshire, the so-called Pindown Inquiry (Levy and Kahan, 1991) and the systematic abuse of young men by a paedophile ring in the residential care system in North Wales (Department of Health, 2000d). Both raise very important and very different issues and if you intend to practise in this area, it is essential for you to be well acquainted with them.

C H A P T E R   S U M M A R Y

This chapter offered you an overview of how the law can be used to promote children's welfare when things go wrong. We started by explaining the importance of the notion of parental responsibility, setting out the ways in which the law determines who has this, how they might share it and what it actually means. This may have seemed an odd starting point, but the law centres on the notion of parents taking responsibility for their children and social workers working in partnership with them, as you saw in the previous chapter. Therefore it was crucial to know who can have parental responsibility and who has the right to participate in decision-making regarding children.

The chapter then summarised the position regarding disputes about the care of children, in what lawyers would call private law family proceedings. In practice, these are dominated by failures to agree over where children should live following the divorce of their parents. As we saw, however, court cases do not exclusively concern themselves with residence, but may also need to consider contact, and securing children's welfare by insisting that certain things be done, or else that they should not be done.

We then proceeded into one of the most demanding areas of professional social work practice: responding to allegations that children have been abused. The chapter considered the underlying principles of the Children Act 1989 as they relate to child protection investigations, and also summarised the system that exists for ensuring that decisions are based on sound evidence and result from effective inter-agency working. There are a number of court orders that may have to be considered in the short term, and we looked at how these related to the final decision-making of the courts concerning care and supervision. In passing, some key principles were underlined in relation to proving the *threshold criteria* and applying the welfare principles enshrined in the legislation. Looking specifically at the court system, we saw that there is provision for separate representation and advocacy for children involved in public law proceedings, and Chapter 7 will say more about the social work role in court.

The chapter concluded by alerting you to examples where the system has, unfortunately, failed children. An extract from the recent Climbié Inquiry was quoted as it resulted in significant changes in the law and practice directions that guide child protection social work.

It is important to state that in some respects we have only really been able to touch the surface of some of the fundamental issues raised in child protection social work. Intending practitioners will need to incorporate what has been learnt here into their skills development work in carrying out assessments, and may also need to refer to more specialist child-care law texts which would provide more detail of the legislation itself and offer guidance in the somewhat complex case law that is relevant to this area. You will find the relevant texts listed overleaf and in the bibliography at the end of the book.

Brammer, A (2007) Social Work Law (2nd edition). Harlow: Pearson. Comprehensive overview of social work law with Part Two dedicated to children and families.

Brayne, H, Martin, G and Carr, H (2005) Law for Social Workers (9th edition). Oxford: Oxford University Press. Comprehensive overview of social work law with eight chapters on social work law relating to children.

Department for Education and Skills (2006b) The Children Act 1989 Report 2004 and 2005. Nottingham: DfES publications. Overview of the operation in practice of all aspects of the Children Act 1989.

Department of Health (2000d) Lost in Care – Report of the Tribunal of Inquiry into the Abuse of Children in Care in the Former County Council Areas of Gwynedd and Clwyd since 1974. London: Stationery Office. Sexual abuse in the residential care system in North Wales.

Department of Health and Home Office (2003) The Victoria Climbié inquiry: report of an inquiry by Lord Laming. London: Stationery Office. Victoria Climbié Inquiry report.

Levy, A and Kahan, B (1991) The Pindown Experience and the Protection of Children – Report of the Staffordshire Child Care Inquiry 1990. Stafford: Staffordshire County Council. Excessive restraint used in residential care; there is also a useful extract in **Brayne, H and Broadbent, G** (2002) Legal Materials for Social Workers. Oxford: Oxford University Press, pp292–299.

SCIE (Social Care Institute for Excellence): Bostock, L, Bairstow, S, Fish, S and Macleod, F (2005) Managing risk and minimizing mistakes in services to children and families. Bristol: Policy Press. By drawing out lessons from the inquiry into the death of Victoria Climbié, this report focuses on the management of risk at an organisational, rather than individual, level.

White, R, Carr, P and Lowe, N (2002) The Children Act in practice (3rd edition). London: Butterworths. Comprehensive practice-related guide to the Children Act 1989 which includes the Act itself and its Regulations.

Climbié Inquiry Report: available at **www.victoria-climbie-inquiry.org.uk/finreport/finreport.htm**

Every Child Matters: Next Steps; Every Child Matters: Change For Children In Social Care; Every Child Matters: Change For Children In Schools: **www.everychildmatters.gov.uk**

Quality Protects: **www.dfes.gov.uk/qualityprotects/**

Social Services Improvement Agency (Wales): general information on children's services: **www.allwalesunit.gov.uk/index.cfm?articleid=5**

Chapter 5

Community care

Introduction

This chapter examines the law as it relates to social work practice in the area of what has come to be known as 'community care'. This refers to all aspects of social work associated with the provision of services for adults although in practice services are offered only to selected groups. Some texts refer to these groups as *vulnerable adults*, meaning groups of people who experience disability or long-term illness or frailty that results in an inability to care for themselves, or have insufficient understanding of their own needs to be able to live safely, possibly at immediate danger of exploitation, or in some cases posing a risk to other people.

The list of standards above indicates rightly that at the heart of community care social work lie the skills of assessment, ability to plan using knowledge of resources to support and empower service users, and a realistic awareness of issues of risk balanced against people's rights of self-determination.

This chapter is therefore quite wide-ranging. It covers:

- the assessment of any adult who believes they need social services;

- the provision of services for adults who fall into specific categories;

- support for carers;

- the protection of vulnerable adults both from themselves and from other people.

What are community care services?

The term 'community care' is a slight misnomer. Outside the field of health and social care, most people would probably assume that community care refers to services that support people by helping them to stay living in their own homes, in their local communities, for as long as they wish. In fact, community care includes residential provision which in many cases may well be very distant from people's 'home' communities. This is an irony to many social work practitioners, but the law is clear that community care covers all those areas other than hospital in-patient care.

Indeed, identifying community care services is more complex than you might presuppose. You would be perfectly entitled to anticipate at this point a list of services that the social services generally (meaning local authorities, health trusts, care trusts, independent organisations and voluntary agencies) can offer to people. Given that this is a book about social work law, you would then expect this to be related to rights and duties: the rights of people to have certain kinds of services, and duties laid on statutory agencies to provide them. We are about to prove that life is not so simple.

The kinds of community care services potentially available to service users depend on the category of person who 'needs' the service. While crude categorisation of people and assumptions about what groups of people collectively need appear to run contrary to some core principles of anti-discriminatory practice, the law can only operate by specifying which groups of people are entitled to which services. In practice there is a hierarchy of entitlement. Some people have greater rights than others; for example, people with disabilities have stronger claims to have their needs assessed than others. So in effect the answer to the question – what are community care services? – actually boils down to a different question: which groups of adults are identified as requiring services to support them in daily living?

ACTIVITY 5.1

If you were a legislator or policymaker, which groups of adults would you identify as being those most likely to need community care services and why?

Draw up a list, indicating some of the reasons why these groups should be offered services. You may find it easier to start this exercise by drawing up the list first. That should take you about ten minutes or so. Thinking through the reasons will take you longer: perhaps 20–30 minutes.

Of course if you have some experience of social work already you will probably have found the first part of this exercise relatively easy, since you are already familiar with which social services are provided and for whom. However, you may not have identified all the groups; and reflecting about why people need community care requires broader thinking.

The primary groups for whom the community care services are provided are as follows:

- People with physical disabilities, referred to in the legislation as *disabled persons* – not a term that is generally considered to accord with social work principles of anti-discriminatory practice (Dalrymple and Burke, 1995), but as this is the phrase used in legislation we will of necessity have to keep to it.

- Older people: nowhere specifically is the age at which someone becomes *older* defined. It might be reasonable to suppose that this would generally be determined by the statutory retirement age, since allocation of national and local resources reflects this, but even this is not an absolute with retirement ages across Europe beginning to creep up. A common sense approach would suggest that priority is accorded to people who are frail or who are affected by loss of faculties that impair their ability to care for themselves.

- People with learning disabilities or learning difficulties, whose needs have been specifically highlighted in the White Paper *Valuing people* (Department of Health, 2001b) and who have been the subject of a major policy shift in the sense that a number of people in this category have been moved from long-stay hospitals through to some kind of community resource (Brown and Smith, 1992).

- People with *mental health problems*, which is a term in social work that refers not just to people with mental 'illness' as such but also extends to people whose ability to function is impaired by various forms of cognitive and behavioural problems. It may be worth noting straight away that the legislation uses a narrower definition of *mental disorder* (section 1 Mental Health Act 1983 and see later discussion in this chapter), whereas the National Service Framework for Mental Health that guides practice (Department of Health, 1999) prefers the broader approach.

As to the reasons why people should have services in the community, you probably listed several times the expectation that people should be helped to continue living in their own homes. In some cases this may be part of the process of rehabilitation from hospital; in others community care may prevent people being admitted to hospital. There is much talk about community care services being necessary to avoid 'bed blocking', that is, people staying in hospital longer than is necessary because of lack of community resources, but this risks moving the focus away from the main purpose of community care which is to provide a comparatively small amount of additional help for people who can no longer perform all the basic care functions for themselves.

As far as the legislation is concerned, service users need to be identified as belonging to particular groups. The following table sets out the main legislation that offers services to these groups. This includes reference to overriding legislation applicable to all, the importance of which was explained in Chapter 2.

Table 5.1 *Legislation most directly relevant to community care*

Group	Specific legislation	Main provisions of legislation	General legislation applicable to all
People with physical disabilities	Chronically Sick and Disabled Persons Act 1970	local authority duty to assess general needs and numbers, provision of specific services	Care Standards Act 2000, Health and Social Care (Community Health and Standards) Act 2003: inspection of homes and services
	Community Care (Direct Payments) Act 1996 Health and Social Care Act 2001	service users can purchase services directly	Community Care (Residential Accommodation) Act 1998: charges for care
			Disability Discrimination Act 1995, Disability Discrimination Act 2005, general anti-discriminatory law
	Disabled Persons (Services, Consultation and Representation) Act 1986	advocacy and rights to involvement in assessment	Disability Rights Commission Act 1999: sets up Commission to implement anti-discriminatory law
	National Assistance Act 1948	service provision including residential care	Equality Act 2006: establishes Commission for Equality and Human Rights, addresses equality and discrimination in relation to gender, disability, sexual orientation, religion, age, race and promotes human rights generally
	National Health Service and Community Care Act 1990	assessment, community care plans, rights of redress	Enduring Power of Attorney Act 1985: enables power of attorney to continue after loss of capacity to consent, to be replaced by lasting power under Mental Capacity Act 2005
People with learning disabilities	none specifically but all disability law could apply	see above	Family Law Act 1996, Domestic Violence, Crime and Victims Act 2004: protection from violence in the home
Older people	Health Services and Public Health Act 1968	specific service provision	Health Act 1999: establishment of care trusts and primary care trusts
	Health and Social Services and Social Security Adjudication Act 1983	local authority duty to charge for services	Health and Social Care Act 2001: direct payments
	National Assistance Act 1948	services generally, including residential care	Human Rights Act 1998: enshrines European Convention on Human Rights into UK law
	National Health Service and Community Care Act 1990	publishing plans, assessment, rights of redress	Local Authority Social Services Act 1970: establishment of local authority social services departments, directs local authorities to obey government circulars
	Commissioner for Older People (Wales) Act 2006	creates Commissioner for Older People to ensure interests of older people in Wales are safeguarded and promoted	Local Government Act 2000: collaboration of public authorities in financing services
			Mental Capacity Act 2005: consent and decision-making
			National Health Service Act 2006, National Health Service (Wales) Act 2006, National Health Service (Consequential Provisions) Act 2006: provision of comprehensive health service, organisation of health and social care services
Carers	Carers (Recognition and Services) Act 1995	carer's right to assessment in tandem with service user	Police and Criminal Evidence Act 1984: life and limb protection
	Carers and Disabled Children Act 2000	independent right to assessment	Race Relations Act 1976: avoidance of discrimination
People with mental health problems	Mental Health Act 1983	hospital admission, treatment, discharge, Court of Protection	Race Relations (Amendment) Act 2000: duty to promote racial harmony and eliminate discrimination
	all legislation applicable to people with disabilities	see above	

While this may be a useful way to begin to clarify the law, there are some important points to make about it.

- People quite often belong to more than one group – for example, older people quite often have disabilities such as arthritis, people can have a combination of learning disabilities and physical disabilities.

- There is a marked difference between groups for whom there appears to be a fair amount of compassion and those who are often perceived as a threat to the rest of society – the obvious example being people with enduring and severe mental health problems (see Chapter 2)

When we examine the range of services offered, you will need to bear in mind the underlying principles whereby local authorities operate. Specifically here four key principles operate.

- Local authorities can only do what the law says they can do – to offer more than this may mean they are acting beyond their powers which would make them liable to legal sanctions such as surcharges.

- Local authorities cannot interfere in people's lives by imposing services on them – there is no such thing as acting in the best interests of adults in the same way that there is in relation to all children and the Children Act 1989, although there is delegated decision-making authority for people who *lack capacity* to consent (section 5 Mental Capacity Act 2005).

- Services should be offered on the basis of assessed need, and not simply on the grounds of what is available – this is often referred to as the *needs led* assessment principle.

- Services are delivered in accordance with general requirements, such as in relation to anti-discriminatory law, as well as specific statutes (see Table 5.1 on p78).

There are some practice implications from this. First and foremost, assessment has to be a first and separate activity conducted before there is a decision about what services are offered. Second, assessment must not be determined by the availability or otherwise of services, although obviously it cannot be conducted entirely in a vacuum. Third, assessment has to centre on what people need, not on what they want. By now you should be familiar with assessment as a key social work task and in Chapter 4 there was a reference to the Framework for Assessment (Department of Health, 2000c) that underpins a great deal of work with children and families. There is no equivalent framework for the assessment of adults, but there are relevant National Service Frameworks (Department of Health, 1999, 2001a) for professionals from different disciplines and there is a movement towards the notion of a single assessment tool to which the different professionals contribute (see Department of Health, 2001a, Standard 2). In determining need, you may find it useful to look at the ways in which people have identified different levels or 'hierarchies' of need (see section on Maslow in Parker and Bradley, 2007). The law itself does not define need, but delegates responsibility for determining level of need to social workers, so it is important for you to understand how needs can be assessed and evaluated.

CASE STUDY

Jaswinder is finding it increasingly difficult to cope with caring for her ageing mother, Arima, who is 86 and described as 'very frail'. Members of her family and her GP suggest that she might approach the social services department and ask them what kind of services they can offer in order to support the family.

Assessment is the key

Assessment is the starting point. Assessment is fundamental to the provision of community care services. Except in emergencies, local authorities cannot offer services, or even arrange services for which they pay, without having first carried out a full assessment of need. Assessment is the task around which everything revolves. Indeed, the key legislation in this area, the National Health Service and Community Care Act 1990, addresses only the provision of information about services, assessment, and service delivery principles. This Act itself says nothing about the kinds of services that might be offered.

The National Health Service and Community Care Act 1990 was passed after some considerable deliberation about the role of local authorities in providing community care services (Cowen, 1999). If at all possible, do read about this since it sets into context the ways in which local authority social services are now organised and why the task of assessment has been separated from service provision. As a result of deliberate policy decisions based on the Report of Sir Roy Griffiths (1988), the National Health Service and Community Care Act 1990 lays on local authorities two key responsibilities: a duty to provide information about services and a duty to assess (sections 46 and 47 National Health Service and Community Care Act 1990). So Jaswinder should have no difficulty getting information about services, although questions may arise about their suitability for people of different cultural backgrounds; naturally one would want this information available in the different languages which people speak in the local community. We don't have space to explore this in depth, but this is one area where local authorities can take the lead in providing culturally sensitive services, ensuring that all needs are met in all areas of the community and generally pursuing the principles of anti-discriminatory practice (of further relevance here may be the general local authority duties to promote equality, enshrined in the Race Relations (Amendment) Act 2000).

The key question however is, having obtained the information about services potentially available, how does Jaswinder access them? After all, she is not actually inquiring about services for herself, but rather services for the family and presumably for her mother that, if provided, would relieve her of some of the burden of care. She could, of course, simply approach the service providers themselves direct and arrange help for which she or her mother would then have to pay. That would be an entirely private arrangement and there is absolutely nothing in the legislation that would prevent them doing this. There would simply be an agreement between the service provider and the service user or, in this case, the carer.

If, however, the family wanted the local authority to pay for the provision of services, which is usually the case, there would have to be an assessment of need first. The assessment of need would be an assessment of Arima Patel's needs, which may not necessarily be focused on the support needs of the carer. For this reason, the Carers (Recognition and Services) Act 1995 extended the duty of assessment to rights of carers to have their needs assessed alongside those of the person for whom they were caring. A difficulty would then arise in some cases where it was not possible to assess the carer's needs because the person being cared for would not agree to any kind of assessment, through lack of understanding, or anxiety about the financial implications of agreeing to services being provided. For this reason the law was extended to offer carers rights to an independent assessment of their current and prospective ability to care for someone (section 1 Carers and Disabled Children Act 2000), and the right to be told about this entitlement even though they may not have requested an independent assessment (section 1 Carers (Equal Opportunities) Act 2004). So in this case Jaswinder does have the right ultimately to ask the local authority for an assessment of her needs as carer, and for consideration of ways in which she can be supported in her caring role.

You also need to be aware that, because of the vagaries of the ways different laws operate, some groups of people have greater entitlements than others. In this instance, people with disabilities are entitled to an assessment (section 4 Disabled Persons (Services, Consultation and Representation) Act 1986), whereas others are simply entitled to request an assessment – a request which presumably the local authority could refuse if on the surface there appeared to be no reason for one.

What services can be provided?

Theoretically, anything anyone would like to provide for anyone else for any reason whatsoever. In a free market, the only real test of the viability of the service is whether there are sufficient customers prepared to pay for it. In community care this is more than just theoretical. Service provision is based on the notion that the independent sector (comprising private and voluntary organisations) has a very real role to play and that people are entitled to purchase any services they require in a 'mixed economy' of care. The key question that concerns potential service users is, of course, money. How do people access services when they cannot afford to do so? It is precisely for this reason that there is a preliminary assessment of need to determine whether people need services and to what extent.

The fundamental question is: what role does the local authority play in the provision of services?

It is very important to keep the sequence right. Assessment comes first. Assessment is an assessment of need; it does not start with services and explore how people might fit into what is available, rather it starts with an assessment of need and then examines the ways in which needs can be met. This should encourage imaginative planning and service development.

CASE STUDY

Mrs Jones lives alone in a house in a tiny village in a rural area. She can just about manage to look after herself except that she can no longer cook. An assessment determines that her only real unmet need is for at least one hot meal a day. Because of the isolation of the village, there is no meals on wheels service. Indeed access to any kind of social services resource is difficult, but there is a pub in the village. The pub provides meals to its customers, and is prepared to enter into a contract to provide Mrs Jones with meals on a regular basis.

In this way Mrs Jones's need is met, although perhaps not quite in the way she may have anticipated! This case study makes the point that there may be a variety of ways of meeting people's needs, and thinking should not be constrained simply by what social services are currently available.

The role of the social worker, then, is to discuss and decide with the service user how their needs can best be met. This means, of course, having a wide knowledge of resources potentially available but also requires an ability to think laterally and imaginatively. The legislation may help here since it does not impose on the local authority the duty to provide services itself directly. The phrase used in the legislation is *arrange for the provision of community care services* which local authorities are authorised to do by making arrangements with service providers in the independent sector if this is appropriate (sections 47 and 48 National Health Service and Community Care Act 1990; for Wales see also Health, Social Care and Wellbeing Strategies (Wales) Regulations 2003). The local authority thereby acquires a 'commissioning' role.

This does not of course stop local authorities from providing services themselves. Acts of Parliament do not actually tell us what services are to be provided. Instead, the principal Acts have specific provisions to enable services to be provided. Reference then needs to be made to regulations, codes of practice, or ministerial directions (for explanation of the differences between these ways of implementing legislation see Chapter 1). In practice, suggestions as to what kind of services local authorities should provide are listed in a number of Local Authority Circulars although in reality these are more than just suggestions: they are expectations, and indications of services that central government is prepared to help finance, and use as benchmarks for awarding star ratings to local authorities.

As we saw earlier, in order to qualify for services people have to belong to certain identified groups. Needs of people with disabilities are addressed primarily through the National Assistance Act 1948 or the Chronically Sick and Disabled Persons Act 1970. Services potentially available under this legislation can be classified as follows:

Services for people with disabilities	Legal authority
Social work support and advice Information about services Recreational facilities Holidays Travel subsidies	section 29 National Assistance Act 1948 as implemented through LAC (93) 10 these are all part of scheme that social services departments must offer (but not all elements are compulsory)
Practical assistance (not defined) Recreational facilities at home Recreational facilities outside the home Holidays Meals Telephones Works of adaptation	section 2 Chronically Sick and Disabled Persons Act 1970: duty to make arrangements for any or all of these
Parking exemption badges	section 21 Chronically Sick and Disabled Persons Act 1970
Residential care	section 21 National Assistance Act 1948: provisions subject to Secretary of State's directions

Services for older people are facilitated by the Health Services and Public Health Act 1968 which sets out (in section 45) a general responsibility to promote their welfare. Directions from the Secretary of State issued subsequently (especially Circular 19/71) lists the kinds of services that a local authority might offer. These include:

- social work support and advice;

- information;

- meals;

- recreation;

- help with travel;

- foster care schemes ('boarding' in the Circular);

- aids and adaptations and similar practical assistance.

In addition older people can be offered residential care under the National Assistance Act 1948 (section 21) and home care and laundry facilities under the National Health Service Act 2006 Schedule 20(3) or National Health Service (Wales) Act 2006 Schedule 15.

Services for people with learning disabilities will be roughly similar to those offered to people who have physical disabilities, and the same legislation will apply. Likewise such services are potentially available to people with mental health problems, if their problems entitle them to be counted as *mentally disordered* in accordance with the definitions of section 1 of the Mental Health Act 1983. This Act lists forms of mental disorder as mental illness, mental impairment, severe mental impairment or psychopathy (for further information on this see Brayne and Carr, 2005, Chapter 18). Section 117 of the Mental Health Act 1983 requires social services departments with health trusts to offer after care services for certain people who have been compulsorily detained in hospital and are being discharged. A legal anomaly has arisen whereby residential charges cannot be levied for services provided under this section 117 (R *v* Manchester City Council, *ex parte* Stennett [2002] UKHL 34).

In order to determine whether someone qualifies as 'disabled' reference needs to be made to section 29 National Assistance Act 1948. Besides people with *mental disorder* this defines a *disabled person* as *blind, deaf or dumb* or *substantially and permanently handicapped by illness, injury, or congenital deformity or such other disabilities as may be prescribed by the Minister* (section 29(1) National Assistance Act 1948).

You will see from this definition that it is rather outmoded, using what in social work terms would be considered highly pejorative language, but nevertheless this is the working legal definition. Note that the person simply has to be entitled to be counted as disabled. They do not have to be registered officially anywhere before qualifying for services. However, local authorities do have a duty to maintain information about people with disabilities and to make plans on the basis of this information. There is a specific duty to ascertain numbers (section 1 Chronically Sick and Disabled Persons Act 1970) and to disseminate information through the annual community care plan (section 46 National Health Service and Community Care Act 1990).

These lists of services are not exhaustive or comprehensive but are intended to cover the main kinds of services offered with indications of the legal authority for doing so (more specialist provision would include examples such as hostel accommodation for training for employment and financial assistance with the provision of wardens).

Commissioning services

This section is headed 'Commissioning services' to emphasise that the social worker's key role is to arrange for the provision of services that meet the needs that have been identified.

> ## CASE STUDY
>
> *Laura has multiple sclerosis. She lives with her partner in a bungalow that generally meets her needs, but in view of a deterioration in her physical condition, she now finds that she needs additional assistance. A full assessment is undertaken and highlights the need for a number of aids and adaptations that would enhance mobility, together with a significant number of hours of home care. The social worker is concerned that if there is a continued deterioration, Laura will get to the position where she needs 24-hour care.*

Laura clearly is entitled to an assessment, but to what extent is she entitled to services as a result of the assessment? What level of services have to be provided?

The answers lies in the assessment itself and its outcome. The law requires the local authority to *make a decision about provision by them* of community care services (section 47 National Health Service and Community Care Act 1990) which in effect means a statement has to be made about the extent to which the local authority is going to meet the assessed needs. Careful phrasing of the law means that the local authority is not automatically directed to meet each and every need it has identified. It certainly does not have to meet those needs itself (see discussion above). However, nor does it mean that the local authority can treat the assessment as a paper exercise; there is a commitment to doing something. Case law confirms this: lack of money to provide services does not excuse a local authority carrying out an assessment (R *v* Bristol City Council, *ex parte* Penfold [1998] CCL Rep 315). All of this underlines the importance of sharing information with service users – which in any case is a legal obligation under the Data Protection Act 1998 – and being careful and precise as to what is stated about service provision on the basis of the assessment. Once you start practising as a student social worker, it would be well worthwhile asking to see policy statements concerning assessments and expectations of agencies concerning the outcome of those assessments.

Commissioning services obviously presupposes knowledge and awareness of what services are potentially available, and inevitably this will vary from area to area. Clearly many of these will be drawn from the list local authorities maintain as part of their community care plans. One issue of concern to service users will inevitably be payments. The law makes it quite clear that there may be a charge for community care services, but not for the assessment, with an expectation that service provision will be means tested (section 22 National Assistance Act 1948, section 17 Health and Social Services and Social Security Adjudication Act 1983). This stands in marked contrast to National Health services which are provided free of charge, and becomes quite problematic when people receive a mixture of medical and social care. It can also encourage redefinition of care so that it becomes medical rather than social.

Each local authority, within government guidelines, determines its own priorities and charging policy so it is not possible to offer a definitive guide but you should be aware of some general principles:

- Determining eligibility for community care services is usually based on assessment of risk to independence if help is not provided, and local authorities are effectively obliged to adopt the Department of Health guidelines Fair Access to Care Services for this purpose as it is linked to circular LAC 2003(13) issued under section 7 of the Local Authority Social Services Act 1970 (Department of Health, 2003b; see also website address at end of chapter). Fair Access to Care Services divides need into four categories: critical, substantial, moderate or low.

- In assessing ability to pay a local authority is entitled to take into account resources rather than simply income – this is important, for example where someone owns their own house but has only a limited income. Nevertheless the local authority cannot take everything, so even if someone receives residential care for several years, there is always a certain amount of capital disregarded (National Assistance (Assessment of Resources) Regulations 1992; Community Care (Residential Accommodation) Act 1998; Health and Social Care Act 2001).

- Services cannot be withdrawn simply because someone is unable to pay and charges should be consistent – if necessary the local authority has to pursue the debt by other legal means and needs to abide by government guidance concerning eligibility for services for recipients of certain benefits (Local Authority Circular LAC 2001(32) and Care Standards Act 2000).

- If the local authority is not prepared to meet the full costs of the service, service users or their relatives can supplement this if they wish – this may well be the case where the family chooses one service in preference to the cheapest which the local authority offers (National Assistance Act 1948 (Choice of Accommodation) Directions 1992; Local Authority Circular 93 (10); Health and Social Care Act 2001).

- Service users have the right in many cases to opt to commission services themselves and in such cases receive the payment for services direct from the local authority thereby enhancing the degree of choice they have (Community Care (Direct Payments) Act 1996; Carers and Disabled Children Act 2000; Health and Social Care Act 2001; Community Care, Services for Carers and Children's Services (Direct Payments) (England) Regulations 2003; Community Care, Services for Carers and Children's Services (Direct Payments) (Wales) Regulations 2004).

One point you may have noticed from the case study is the possibility of Laura needing 24-hour care. What happens if the local authority decides that residential care is cheaper than round-the-clock care in the person's own home? Here we return to the point made earlier about residential care being considered a community care service and so, contrary to what one might assume, offering residential care is acceptable. The fact that the service user and family are not entirely in favour, and that it seems to undermine the principle of keeping people living in their own localities, has to be set against what is cost-effective and the local authority is perfectly entitled to go for this option (R *v* Lancashire County Council, ex parte Ingham [1995] QBD CO 774; Clements, 1996, p59).

What of the quality of the services provided? Commissioners of services undoubtedly have some responsibility for this but in addition there is provision for inspection and complaints procedures.

CASE STUDY

Daphne Meadows is very dissatisfied with Beechwood Lodge where she has been living for the last eight months. Despite the home's claim to offer high-quality care, Daphne feels that it falls short in two respects: there is insufficient staffing and she is still compelled to share a room with another resident despite a promise that she would have a room to herself.

In which case she can, of course, complain. She can complain direct to the managers of the home and, if the placement was arranged through the local authority, she can complain to them. Community care legislation sets out a precise complaints procedure that moves complaints gradually up through the hierarchy of the social services (section 50 National Health Service and Community Care Act 1990; Local Authority Social Services Complaints (England) Regulations 2006; Social Services Complaints Procedures (Wales) Regulations 2005). She can also complain to the Commission for Social Care Inspection or the Care and Social Services Inspectorate Wales, responsible under the Care Standards Act 2000 (amended by the Health and Social Care (Community Health and Standards) Act 2003) for registering and inspecting residential homes. The responsibilities of the inspection bodies specifically include management, staffing and facilities. For further information see Chapter 8.

Withdrawing services

Once the local authority agrees to provide services, and services are then provided, can they be withdrawn? Naturally if the service user's needs change, and everyone agrees that they have changed, then withdrawing services is unproblematic. However, consider the following case study which, on this occasion, is a real case.

CASE STUDY

Mr Barry was in his late seventies. He had suffered a stroke and his vision was poor. Gloucestershire social services department had assessed his needs and on this basis provided home care and laundry services. A considerable time after providing the services, the local authority ran into budgetary difficulties and decided to cut community care services 'across the board', reducing home care and withdrawing the home laundry service. So Mr Barry's level of service provision was reduced considerably. He went to court arguing that the local authority's actions were unreasonable and wrong in that his assessed needs had not changed so how could services be reduced.
(R v Gloucestershire County Council, ex parte Barry [1997] 2 WLR 459)

The courts decided that Mr Barry was right, at least up to a point. He should not have had his services withdrawn since there was no basis on which to change the level of services offered as his assessed needs had not changed. However, and unfortunately for Mr Barry, the court declared that it was open for the local authority to reassess his needs on the basis of the new financial situation in which it found itself. In other words it could set new eligibility criteria for services, assess Mr Barry by these criteria, and then presumably explain to Mr Barry how he failed to meet them. Nevertheless the message is loud and clear: services cannot be withdrawn unless there is a reassessment of need.

What if someone is in residential care and the home closes? Surely that is a withdrawal of service? This is precisely the issue that has occurred in a number of cases.

Case decisions

- In *R v North East Devon Health Authority,* ex parte *Coughlan (2000) 51 BMLR 1* the courts decided that the decision of the health authority to close a home breached Article 8 of the European Convention.
- In *R (on the application of Bodimeade and others) v London Borough of Camden (2001) EWHC Admin 271* the local authority Social Services Committee's decision to close a home was quashed.
- In *Cowl v Plymouth City Council (2002) 1 WLR 803* the local authority decision to close a home was upheld.
- In *R v Servite Houses* ex parte *Goldsmith (2001) LGR 55* it was declared that a housing association is not subject to public law. Likewise in *R (on the application of Heather and others) v Leonard Cheshire Foundation (2001) 2 All ER 936* it was decided by the court that a voluntary organisation was not subject to the Human Rights Act 1998. So in these cases the court had no jurisdiction to review decisions on the grounds of potential breaches of the European Convention on Human Rights.
- In *R (on the application of Madden and others) v Bury Metropolitan Borough Council (2002) EWHC (Admin) 1882,* the residents of Warthfield Residential Home persuaded the courts that the authority's decision to close the home was unlawful as the authority owed the claimants a duty to act fairly, and fairness in that case required consultation.
- In *R (on the application of Goldsmith) v London Borough of Wandsworth (2004) EWCA Civ 1170,* the decision to move a woman from residential care to nursing care was quashed by the court as the Local Continuing Care Panel had failed to produce reasons and failed to consider a community care assessment.
- In *R (on the application of S and another v Leicester City Council (2004) EWHC (Admin) 533,* the local authority's decision to move the applicant from her preferred accommodation was quashed as a formal assessment of needs should have been carried out.
- More generally courts have confirmed that breaches of duty to provide appropriate accommodation under section 21 of the National Assistance Act 1948 may possibly be breaches of the European Convention on Human Rights Article 8 (for example in *R (on the application of Bernard) v Enfield London BC [2003] HLR 354).*

You may be wondering why the decisions in these cases vary and what they have to do with the European Convention on Human Rights. If you recall from Chapter 2, Article 8 concerns the right to family life and therefore by implication people's rights to be protected from arbitrary decisions to close the home in which they live. The principle behind this is that residents should have a 'home for life' and should not be required to move without agreement just because public authorities say so. Effectively, what the courts are saying is that decisions to close homes should be taken in consultation with residents and proper notice given. The Health Authority or social services department should make alternative plans in conjunction with service users, and work towards an agreement to move elsewhere. However, the courts have also decided that the Human Rights Act 1998 which implements the European Convention does not apply to the independent sector and so, in effect, residents in homes run by private or charitable organisations do not have the same rights of consultation and preparation for closure as those in public authority care.

Protecting vulnerable adults

ACTIVITY **5.2**

Consider the following questions:

- *In what ways might vulnerable adults need protection?*
- *What are the ethical issues that arise when social workers try to take action to protect vulnerable adults?*

In considering the first question, you probably started by thinking of ways in which vulnerable adults could be abused by other people and may have therefore started with physical protection. This may have triggered thoughts about how people sometimes need to be protected from themselves, and how sometimes they appear to be in need of removal from a situation which is dangerous to them. Hopefully, it will also have occurred to you that some adults are very vulnerable to exploitation by others, especially with regard to their finances. This section considers each of these areas very briefly before concluding with a consideration of some the ethical issues that arise.

Elder abuse, as it is sometimes called, is a topic that has attracted an increasing amount of attention over recent years (Eastman, 1994; Pritchard, 2001). This interest on the part of social workers has now been translated into policy and procedures that direct the attention of practitioners to the whole issue of the abuse of vulnerable adults (Department of Health, 2000e). This, of course, is not confined to older people. The law makes it clear that any physical assault is a criminal offence, but the issue for vulnerable adults is that quite often they may have difficulties, because of fear or diminished intellectual abilities, recording precisely what happened and who did what to them. It is for this reason that prosecutions for abuse of older people or people with learning disabilities are extremely rare. The Crown Prosecution Service has to be concerned with the probability of securing a conviction and vulnerable adults do not make very good prosecution witnesses. However, there have recently been moves to enhance the potential for vulnerable adults providing credible and reliable evidence in court (Home Office, 1998, 2002a; see also websites at the end of this chapter).

Most would agree that, in the small minority of cases where the carer is implicated in the abuse, prosecution is rarely a successful way of addressing abuse since in many cases the abuser is under stress due to an excess of caring responsibilities. In all cases an appropriate approach may be to call a case conference so as to agree a strategy for protecting the vulnerable person. The Department of Health has issued guidelines to local authorities that suggests that they have a key co-ordinating role in this (Department of Health, 2000e) although you should note that the potential legal safeguards for vulnerable adults are far fewer than those available to children. There is no equivalent of care orders for vulnerable adults and no duty on local authorities to investigate abuse equivalent to section 47 Children Act 1989.

A common situation in social work is a clamour for someone to be removed from their home on the grounds that they are at considerable risk of harming themselves. They do not appear to understand the dangers they incur by leaving the gas on, by lighting fires or by failing to eat properly, for example. However, those who press for immediate action often fail to realise that there is no law that authorises people simply to be 'taken away' or 'put into care'. There are just three pieces of legislation that in some way permit compulsory removal of adults.

The first is a very rarely used section of the National Assistance Act 1948 which allows the removal of someone *suffering from grave chronic disease or, being aged, infirm or physically incapacitated... living in insanitary conditions* and not receiving *proper care and attention* (section 47 National Assistance Act 1948). This is not really about the interests of the vulnerable but more with a view to preventing them being a sanitation hazard to others. It is not a direct concern to social workers since the applicant is usually a medical officer of health. In practice the potential for using this is constrained since there are so many ethical objections, not least of which is that it is probably a direct contravention of the European Convention on Human Rights (Brammer, 2007, pp551–552).

The second piece of legislation involves the police. There is a general police power that allows officers to enter and search premises if this is necessary in order to save *life and limb* (section 17(1) Police and Criminal Evidence Act 1984). This may be helpful in circumstances where a vulnerable adult is obviously in need of urgent medical attention, perhaps lying on the floor in their locked home. This legislation could be used to enable police to force entry, and common law powers would then enable them to take the vulnerable adult to hospital: this would be seen as a reasonable action that prevents the threat to life, an action authorised by common law.

The only other legislation that permits compulsory removal is the Mental Health Act 1983. This does directly involve social workers, in this case Approved Social Workers who have a special responsibility and special training for dealing with people with mental 'disorders'. Space does not permit an examination of this Act in detail but suffice it to say that it does allow for people to be admitted and detained in hospital where they are or may be suffering from a mental disorder, and they need to be detained in the interests of their own health, or safety or for the protection of other people. We explored some of these issues in Chapter 2. The issue that arises in practice with vulnerable adults is that they may fail to qualify for consideration as mentally disordered. Someone with dementia, for example, may or may not be described as suffering from a mental illness. Likewise people with learning disabilities are not necessarily *mentally impaired* since the Mental Health Act requires mental *impairment* to be *associated with abnormally aggressive or seriously irresponsible conduct* (section 1(2) Mental Health Act 1983).

As regards financial abuse and responsibility for personal financial affairs generally, it is important to note that this needs to be addressed quite separately from community care legislation. The law assumes that people are fully entitled to do what they wish with their money and if they choose to give it away then that is their absolute right. The unscrupulous can easily exploit this situation, but in some cases the vulnerable adult clearly does not have the capacity to understand what they are doing with their money.

The two legal processes for social workers to consider here are Power of Attorney and the Court of Protection. A Power of Attorney is an authority for one person to ask another to look after their financial affairs, but in law it ceases as soon as the person granting authority becomes too confused (technically *incapacitated*) to give full consent to the arrangement. To address this the Enduring Power of Attorney Act 1985 and subsequently the Mental Capacity Act 2005 were introduced. The 1985 Act allowed someone to declare from the start that they wished the Power of Attorney to continue even though they lost the capacity to consent to it, and the Mental Capacity Act 2005 (section 9) takes this a stage further, extending financial powers to personal welfare under a comprehensive Lasting Power of Attorney (Lasting Powers replace Enduring Powers). This is an excellent course of action providing people know in advance that lack of capacity to manage affairs is likely. In practice there is more often a situation where someone has already become *incapacitated*. Here the only recourse is to the Court of Protection which will take over people's financial affairs if necessary and administer them through a court-appointed deputy. Deputies can take decisions on welfare, health and finance as authorised by the Court but will not be able to refuse consent to life-sustaining treatment (section 11 Mental Capacity Act 2005). One consideration worth bearing in mind is that whilst the court will take over all financial aspects, so effectively barring any possibility of exploitation, there will be fees payable.

The Court of Protection derives its authority (from October 2007) from Part 2 of the Mental Capacity Act 2005, operating through the Public Guardian (sections 45–61 Mental Capacity Act 2005), with rights for vulnerable people to access independent Mental Capacity Advocates to represent their wishes, feelings, beliefs and values as well as challenging decisions (sections 35–41 Mental Capacity Act 2005).

Now to the ethical issues. How many of these did you identify?

As regards physical abuse, the principal concern may be the extent to which it is hidden and so, in seeking out potential abuse, the social worker may be violating some key principles. First of these is consent and the rights of an adult to resist an investigation into abuse. It may seem strange that someone would be reluctant to be protected from abuse, but don't forget that there is a possibility that the abuser is a close and normally trusted relative and someone on whom the abused person is utterly dependent. In children's cases it is legally justified to intervene whether the child consents or not. The issue with adults is quite different. Adults have rights to be informed, an entitlement to have their say as to whether an investigation proceeds and there is no equivalent of care proceedings. You can doubtless see that in many cases this poses a dilemma, especially where it is debatable whether the older person really understands the situation fully. This is particularly an issue with people with dementia.

This leads on to the second ethical issue that concerns the capacity of people to give reliable evidence, which may limit the extent to which abuse can be fully investigated. This does not refer solely to the potential for court proceedings, which are rare, but rather to the wider issue of what steps can be legitimately taken and on what basis.

Extending this to the issue of compulsory intervention, matters become very problematic. Not only is there the whole ethical issue about depriving people of their fundamental rights to self-determination, there is the associated legal issue that this may well infringe their basic rights as enshrined in the European Convention. There is also the very real practice issue that arises in such cases, namely will any good be achieved by forcibly removing someone from their home? Social workers need to balance the anxiety of leaving people in their own homes against the very real risk of premature death associated with forcible removal from home.

Finally it may be worth thinking about whether, in the desire to protect vulnerable adults, social workers may inadvertently be acting oppressively. There is an underlying assumption that in pushing for the kinds of procedures outlined by the Department of Health (2000e) and the Association of Directors of Social Services (2005), this whole area of work is moving towards an approach that is similar to child care social work. Yet the issues are very different. We are here dealing with adults, who have absolute rights to make their own choices

(Williams, 2002). In cases where they are unable to give informed consent, it may not be adequate simply to assume that other people can 'take over'. Rather what may be needed is greater clarity about the point at which someone becomes incapable of making their own decisions or managing their own affairs, and an acceptance that the extent to which people can give consent may vary. In this respect the Mental Capacity Act 2005 may be helpful, for it starts with a presumption that someone has capacity unless proved otherwise; that people must be supported to make their own decisions as far as is practicable; that people are entitled to make unwise decisions; but where someone else makes decisions for vulnerable adults, they must do so in their 'best interests' adopting the 'least restrictive' option wherever possible (sections 1–4 Mental Capacity Act 2005). Furthermore, the Mental Capacity Act 2005 (section 37) recognises the need for independent mental capacity advocates (IMCAs) for people who have no family or friends where serious issues are being decided, which might include provision of community care services. This issue of independent advocacy was originally addressed by the Law Commission (1993) but it has taken a long time for legislation to be forthcoming. If you practise in this area, do note that the Act, fully operational from the end of 2007, is to be interpreted by reference to a Code of Practice (Department of Constitutional Affairs, 2007) which you will need to consult.

Experiencing community care

The Joseph Rowntree Foundation (for website address see end of chapter) has published a considerable amount of research on community care, much of it incorporating a carer and user perspective. Some of this has direct relevance to the legally related practice issues examined in this chapter. For example:

RESEARCH SUMMARY

In 1994 researchers conducted a study of older people who returned to the community after a stroke. This research demonstrated that a majority of users had only a vague perception of the care management and community care service delivery processes.
(Baldock and Ungerson, 1994)

In 1998 researchers examined the experiences of relatives when a frail older person sought admission to a care home. This revealed that carers found choosing a suitable home an intimidating process; they were frustrated by social workers' reticence about making recommendations and were surprised to discover that the costs of long-term care would not be met by the NHS. In several cases only after admission did families realise costs would be imposed and means tested.
(Wright, 1998)

In 2001, researchers studied older people's experience of home care and community care more generally. Service users valued consistency of support, flexibility in responding to needs and, in the case of ethnic minority groups, culturally sensitive services (for example, specific foods and activities in day-care centres). Service users would welcome regular reviews of the quality of services provided.
(Raynes et al., 2001)

RESEARCH SUMMARY

In 2002, researchers asked about advocacy for black and minority ethnic users and carers. This uncovered a great deal of dissatisfaction with mainstream mental health services. There was a lack of awareness of advocacy services, but service users and carers felt most empowered when they had an advocate who reflected their culture, gender and ethnicity. (Rai-Atkins et al., 2002)

Finally, also in 2002, researchers studied support services for Asian disabled people. Low take-up of community care services amongst Asian people was related to a lack of confidence in community care service providers. The reason for this distrust was clearly connected to a limited understanding of, and response to, cultural and religious differences. Several disabled service users felt discriminated against, pointing to a lack of provision for their religious and cultural needs. The consequence of this was isolation and forced dependency on families. (Vernon, 2002)

The whole issue of user and carer empowerment is, of course, of great importance (Sharkey, 2000). From the point of view of using the law, three key issues are worth highlighting from this in our conclusion: co-ordination and integration of services; financial arrangements; and empowerment in the context of anti-discriminatory practice.

Integrating health and social care, finance, and empowering service users and carers

A key issue for the future of community care practice is the move towards greater integration of health and social services. For a long time it has been realised that from a user perspective the divide between health and social care can appear to be arbitrary – for example, often there is no essential difference between what community psychiatric nurses and mental health social workers do when dealing with people with mental health problems. Yet the financial implications of the difference for some service users are considerable: in England and Wales nursing care is free, but social care has to be paid for and is means tested. Another negative consequence of the divide is lack of co-ordination of services and inconsistencies in assessment. A persistent complaint from carers is that professionals do not know what each other is doing and so service users receive a patchy service, as we saw in the 1994 survey of older people cited above.

To address lack of co-ordination for individual service users, the National Service Framework for Older People (Department of Health, 2001a) promotes the notion of *the single assessment process*. This is an important development whereby social work assessments are integrated into an overall assessment that includes health care assessments and therefore builds up one overall, hopefully consistent and integrated, personal assessment. The aim is simple:

> *To ensure that older people are treated as individuals and they receive appropriate and timely packages of care which meet their needs as individuals, regardless of health and social services boundaries.*
> (Department of Health, 2001a, Standard 2)

92

This objective is to be attained through integrated commissioning arrangements and provision of services, facilitated by changes in funding and administrative arrangements contained in the Health Act 1999 (and subsequently the National Health Service Act 2006 and the National Health Service (Wales) Act 2006), including the creation of Care Trusts, which are NHS organisations to which local authorities can delegate health-related functions (section 45 Health and Social Care Act 2001).

The thorny question of financing long-term care was examined by a Royal Commission (Sutherland, 1999). This recommended payment of social care services through general taxation after an assessment of need. The report has yet to become policy in England and Wales, although the equivalent recommendations for Scotland have been accepted in principle and implemented. This creates an anomaly and perpetuates a system in England and Wales whereby a fine distinction has to be made between services that are medical, and therefore free, and those that are 'care' and may be chargeable, with some clarification offered by the Health and Social Care Act 2001 and Health and Social Care (Community Health and Standards) Act 2003. The Community Care (Delayed Discharges, etc.) Act 2003 implies an acknowledgement that there is a consequent problem in transferring people to providing care services, but addresses this by introducing a system of fines levied on local authorities where there is a delay in transferring people who are occupying hospital beds (so-called 'bed-blockers').

The Green Paper issued in 2005 (Department of Health, 2005) set out a number of proposals that moved the whole debate a stage further, with proposals to integrate and co-ordinate voluntary sector services as well as income support, health services and adult social services. To achieve this there would be a better trained social care workforce, together with an acknowledgement of risks created by greater independence, so that services become *person-centred, proactive and seamless*. The subsequent White Paper, *Our Health, Our Care, Our Say* (Department of Health, 2006b), reaffirmed an increased emphasis on service user choice, direct payments and carer support, arguing strongly for better integration of services with comprehensive long-term reform proposals for both health and social care. There are similar long-term proposals for Wales (Vision 2015, see websites at the end of this chapter) building on integration that has been under way since 2003 (Welsh Assembly, 2003).

As to the specific issue of enpowerment and lack of attention to cultural and religious needs, we need to use the law imaginatively and creatively.

ACTIVITY 5.3

Given the issues highlighted by the research, in what way can the law potentially be used to promote empowerment and inclusive community care services?

Write down measures that you think can be adopted in order to achieve this aim. Try to keep to procedures and processes that actually exist. You may find it helpful to discuss this issue with others and even to ask service providers what measures they adopt.

Some suggestions are to be found in the Exercise Answers, pp147–148, but do note that the law cannot compel people to become good practitioners. All the law can do is facilitate and enhance good practice in ways that you have now explored.

C H A P T E R   S U M M A R Y

In this chapter, you were introduced to the concept of community care and offered an overview of services for adults who might need them. Assessment of need was identified as the central task of social workers. The legal basis for the provision of services was summarised together with the commissioning role of the local authority and service users' rights of redress. The chapter then explored the protection of vulnerable adults, an issue that highlights the ethical dilemmas of promoting independence yet ensuring people's safety and protecting them from others, and others from them. Finally, the chapter cited some examples from research of service users' and carers' perspectives, and used this as a basis for indicating actual and potential changes in policy and the law. It concluded by inviting you to think about ways in which the law can be used to promote user and carer empowerment in accessing quality services.

As a postscript, it needs to be said that one key deficiency of the law is the lack of a comprehensive legal framework. The delivery of community care services and protection of vulnerable adults would be improved immeasurably if legislation could be brought together into a consolidating Act, like the Children Act 1989. Although reforms such as the Mental Capacity Act 2005 and integration of health and social care services set out in the 2006 White Paper go some way towards achieving this, the current arrangements are still experienced by many as piecemeal, confusing, inconsistent and not at all 'user friendly'.

FURTHER READING

Johns, R and Sedgwick, A (1998) *Law for social work practice: working with vulnerable adults.* Basingstoke: Macmillan. For more comprehensive coverage of community care law in practice (but note some legislation now updated).

Pritchard, J (ed) (2001) *Good practice with vulnerable adults.* London: Jessica Kingsley.

Sharkey, P (2006) *The essentials of community care: a guide for practitioners* (2nd edition). Basingstoke: Macmillan. Good for exploring practice issues related to working with vulnerable adults and community care in current legal context.

Williams, J (2002) Public law protection of vulnerable adults: the debate continues, so does the abuse. *Journal of Social Work* 2(3): 293–316. Argues the case for a new kind of legislation to protect vulnerable adults. Connects this to the Human Rights Act 1998, suggesting that the European Convention on Human Rights poses an obligation on the government to protect vulnerable adults. Includes international comparisons.

WEBSITES

Crown Prosecution Service initiative on vulnerable witnesses and victims of crime: **www.cps.gov.uk/victims_witnesses/index.html**

Disability Rights: **www.direct.gov.uk/en/DisabledPeople/index.htm**

Joseph Rowntree Foundation: **www.jrf.org.uk/**

Legislation: **www.opsi.gov.uk/legislation/uk.htm**

Public Guardianship Office: **www.guardianship.gov.uk**

Social care (England)

Charging for residential accommodation:
www.dh.gov.uk/en/Policyandguidance/Organisationpolicy/Financeandplanning/Residential care/index.htm

Direct payments:
www.dh.gov.uk/en/Policyandguidance/Organisationpolicy/Financeandplanning/Directpaym ents/index.htm

Fair Access to Care Services:
www.dh.gov.uk/en/Publicationsandstatistics/Publications/PublicationsPolicyAndGuidance/ DH_4009653

National Service Framework for Older People:
www.dh.gov.uk/en/Publicationsandstatistics/Publications/PublicationsPolicyAndGuidance/ DH_4003066

Protecting vulnerable adults:
www.dh.gov.uk/en/Policyandguidance/Healthandsocialcaretopics/Socialcare/Vulnerableadu lts/index.htm

Social care (Wales)

Charging for social services: **new.wales.gov.uk/topics/health/socialcare/chargingforsocialser- vices/?lang=en**

Direct payments: **new.wales.gov.uk/topics/health/socialcare/direct_payments/?lang=en**

National Service Framework for Older People in Wales: **www.wales.nhs.uk/sites3/documents/439/ NSFforOlderPeopleInWalesEnglish.pdf**

Protection of vulnerable adults: **new.wales.gov.uk/topics/health/socialcare/protectionofvulnera bleadults/?lang=en**

Vision 2015:
new.wales.gov.uk/about/strategy/strategypublications/designedforlife/vision2015/?lang=en

Chapter 6
Youth justice

Introduction

In England and Wales, social workers play an important part in the youth justice system. Many of them are members of multidisciplinary teams, generally called Youth Offending Teams, which have a key role in preventing offences being committed by young people, writing reports on offenders, implementing various court orders, and supervising offenders on their discharge from custody. In Scotland and Northern Ireland, social workers are potentially involved in the entire criminal justice system, including work with adults and adult mentally ill offenders. The reason for this is historical: there has never been a separate probation service in Scotland, whereas in England and Wales (and Northern Ireland) the probation service has been run as an entirely separate enterprise. Because probation training in England and Wales is now so very different from social work training, it has been decided not to include work with adult offenders in this book. Therefore the focus in this chapter is exclusively on social work with young people who are likely to commit, or have committed, criminal offences (*offending behaviour*).

The local authority has a key role in youth justice, co-ordinating and managing multidisciplinary teams of workers, drawn from the police, probation, education and social work, and these teams are seen as the linchpin of the whole system (section 38 Crime and Disorder Act 1998). This area of social work attracts people who want to work alongside colleagues from other professions in order to help young people become law-abiding citizens and make a positive contribution to society. Youth justice social workers need the skills and knowledge that enable them to work under the direction of the criminal justice and court system in implementing a whole number of court orders. The list of relevant occupational standards reflects this.

The government's national objectives for Youth Offending Teams and the youth justice system generally are:

- the swift administration of justice so that every young person accused of breaking the law has the matter resolved without delay;

- confronting young offenders with the consequences of their offending, for themselves and their family, their victims and the community, and helping them develop a sense of personal responsibility;

- interventions which tackle the particular factors that put a young person at risk of offending and which strengthen 'protective factors';

- punishment proportionate to the seriousness and persistence of offending;

- encouraging reparation to victims by young offenders;

- reinforcing the responsibilities of parents.
(Home Office, 2001)

Rather than just summarise the way the youth justice system puts these ambitions into effect, this chapter will offer a number of short case scenarios that demonstrate the ways in which youth justice social workers operate under the various pieces of legislation. The chapter addresses the following areas:

- preventing crime;

- arrest and bail;

- dealing with first offenders;

- community sentences;

- custody;

- special kinds of orders.

The chapter concludes with an invitation for you to research user perspectives on the way the criminal justice system operates.

Preventing crime

Every local authority must work towards the reduction of crime and disorder and to that end produce an annual youth justice plan (sections 17 and 40 Crime and Disorder Act 1998). The emphasis on preventing crime is made explicit by section 37 Crime and Disorder Act 1998 which talks about preventing *offending by children and young persons*. Yet at the same time courts with whom Youth Offending Teams work must pay attention to the welfare needs of children (section 44 Children and Young Persons Act 1933).

There is also the requirement to act fairly which is not just a requirement on the Youth Justice Board, whose task is to oversee the national scheme of Youth Offending Teams, but is also a general duty in relation to race for most public bodies (Race Relations Amendment Act 2000). Section 95 Criminal Justice Act 1991 refers to the duty of those involved in the criminal justice system to avoid discriminating against anyone *on the ground of race or sex or any other improper ground*.

All of this argues powerfully for awareness of equality issues and incorporation of social work's anti-discriminatory practice values into the work of Youth Offending Teams. The inclusion of social workers in Youth Offending Teams is also essential since they provide the link into other areas of local authority social work with children and families, a connection that is strengthened by the Department of Health's Quality Protects Programme (Department of Health, 2000a). This establishes objectives for improving the care of *looked after* children including a reduction in their offending rate (it is, though, policy rather than law).

CASE STUDY

Family X are generally regarded in their neighbourhood as the 'family from hell'. What particularly irks the neighbours is the fact that the younger children in the family – Terry aged 9 and Jack aged 8 – are often seen engaging in acts of serious vandalism, such as breaking windows in people's homes and throwing stones at passing cars.

Yet Terry and Jack are under the age of criminal responsibility, which in England and Wales is 10. The law assumes that only when children attain this age are they able to distinguish between right and wrong. However, the law now assumes that on their tenth birthdays all children can distinguish between what is lawful and what is criminal (the Crime and Disorder Act 1998 abolished the notion of *doli incapax* whereby the prosecution had to prove that children under 14 knew the difference between right and wrong).

So if they cannot be prosecuted for committing criminal offences, can anything be done? The Crime and Disorder Act 1998 introduced some novel, but so far comparatively rarely used, provisions. Section 11 of the Act refers to child safety orders for which the local authority can apply in the Family Proceedings Courts (different kinds of courts are covered in the next chapter). One of the grounds is that an act has been committed that would have been an offence had the child been 10 or over (another ground is breach of a curfew order – see discussion in next case study). Note, however, that the civil rather than criminal degree of proof (*balance of probabilities* as opposed to *beyond reasonable doubt*) applies to the offence allegation. The purpose of the child safety order is to enforce supervision for up to 12 months with requirements such as avoiding certain places or attending special assessment sessions to address offending behaviour.

It is now two years later. Terry and Jack are therefore aged 11 and 10 respectively. Their behaviour still causes a great deal of concern and anguish.

There are a number of different courses of action that could be taken. For comparatively low level anti-social behaviour, an acceptable behaviour contract could be drawn up by the Youth Offending Team, whereby the two boys (and their parents) agreed to stop the nuisance behaviour and address neighbours' concerns. If this failed, or if the anti-social behaviour were more serious, the local district council (not the children's services authority) or the police could apply for an anti-social behaviour order (ASBO; section 1 Crime and Disorder Act 1998). The local authority should be consulted about the intention to apply for such orders and a social worker should then make an assessment of needs under the Children Act 1989. The grounds for the order basically concern harassment, alarm or distress; nowhere is this defined, although clearly it ought not to derive solely from the fact that people have different cultural norms. ASBOs were rarely used when they were first introduced, and there are doubts as to whether they would conform to the European Convention on Human Rights. However their operation has now been strengthened by the Anti-Social Behaviour Act 2003. Orders last for a minimum of two years and can last indefinitely. They can be supplemented by an Individual Support Order, lasting for up to six months, which compels the young person to address their behaviour (section 322 Criminal Justice Act 2003). Although no criminal conviction for the original behaviour is required – yet it does have to be proved *on the balance of probabilities* – breaching orders is very serious and can lead to imprisonment or fines.

Where children are subject to child safety orders, anti-social behaviour orders or convicted of an offence, the court may also order parents to attend guidance sessions for a period of three months extendable to 12 months (parenting orders), providing such sessions exist in their area (section 8 Crime and Disorder Act 1998). Once sections 23–25 of the Police and Justice Act 2006 are implemented, it will be possible for local authorities and registered social landlords to enter into parenting contracts and apply for parenting orders.

If the district council concludes that there really is a wider problem with the behaviour of children in general in this area, it is possible for them to apply for a general local child curfew (section 14 Crime and Disorder Act 1998, not to be confused with individual curfew orders) which would have the effect of allowing the police to take a child home if found on the streets after certain hours stipulated in the order. These orders can last up to 90 days and are renewable.

Arrest and bail

Because of the piecemeal development of legislation, these procedures mainly apply to young people under 17, whereas the jurisdiction of the Youth Courts and sentences for young offenders apply up to age 18.

Samantha, aged 15, decides to take the day off school and go shopping or rather, for the first time in her life, shoplifting. She is caught by a store detective stealing a couple of items of clothing. The police are called. She is arrested and taken to the police station.

When someone like Samantha who is aged 10–16 is arrested by the police, they should normally be interviewed about that offence in the presence of an *appropriate adult*. Most often this will be a parent, but where the local authority *accommodates* the young person it could be their own social worker. In some cases the Youth Offending Team will be asked to perform this function since provision of *appropriate adults* is one of their official functions. The requirements of the role are set out in the Code of Practice established by section 66 Police and Criminal Evidence Act 1984 as amended by the Serious Organised Crime and Police Act 2005. Specific training is needed to undertake this task so it is not covered in detail here (it is comprehensively covered in Brayne and Carr, 2005, Chapter 5). Suffice to say that appropriate adults are not legal advisers and those arrested have additional rights to have solicitors present when being interviewed.

Once Samantha has been arrested and interviewed in the presence of the appropriate adult, what happens next? Assuming that the police think that there is enough evidence that Samantha committed the offence they have a number of options.

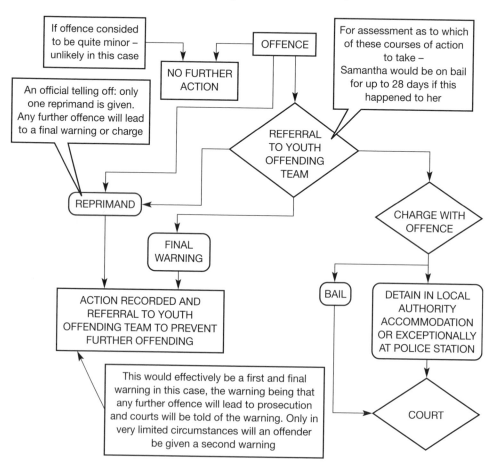

The police have discretion as to where the reprimand or final warning may be administered; it no longer has to be at the police station, but must be in the presence of the *appropriate adult*. A final warning is also treated as an automatic referral to the Youth Offending Team who must then try to instigate a programme to prevent further offences (yet this cannot be imposed on the offender).

If the police decide to charge someone with an offence, they then have to decide what should happen before the person appears in court. The Bail Act 1976 indicates that there should always be a presumption in favour of someone being bailed rather than held in custody and, naturally, there are additional safeguards in relation to young people. The expectation is that the young person would be bailed unconditionally, that is, simply told to report to the court on a particular date and time without having any specific conditions imposed in the meantime. If it appears likely that a young offender would not do this, or might commit further offences, or interfere with witnesses, or has previously breached bail conditions, or 'needs' protection or welfare, bail can be refused (section 38 Police and Criminal Evidence Act 1984). In these cases young people would generally be *accommodated*. Occasionally the police may detain a young person in their custody overnight, but must then bring them before the next available court and explain their reasons for doing so to the court.

When someone appears in court for the first time, the court must either hear the case or adjourn it until it can be heard. During the adjournment, the offender will usually be bailed, either with or without conditions. Courts have some specific bail options available for young people. They may be so concerned about their welfare that they think that at this stage there should be some support and advice offered, and for this reason one of the functions of the Youth Offending Team is to offer a bail support scheme. These are not always run by the teams themselves, but may be projects run by social workers within a local authority or through voluntary agencies. You may be interested to look at some of the research into Bail Supervision and Support schemes in England and Wales. Here are some very brief key points from the evaluation published by the Youth Justice Board for England and Wales (2005).

PRACTICE EXAMPLE *1*

Bail Supervision and Support schemes

*Nacro Cymru analysed 11,393 records of young people referred to or receiving services ....
Of referrals to schemes, 89 per cent were male and 11 per cent female. Seventeen-year-old males made up the biggest single group of young people at 32 per cent, and 79 per cent of referrals were identified as White British.*

The length of programmes varied, depending on the seriousness and complications of the case and the working of courts in the area. The majority of bail programmes were for four weeks or less (55 per cent), making any long-term change in the young person's circumstances difficult to achieve.

Fifty-five per cent fully complied with their bail supervision programme. These were identified as young people who had not re-offended (measured in terms of arrest and charge) or been reported to the police as being in breach of their bail supervision programme or any other bail condition. In addition, they would have attended all court appearances during the bail supervision period. The main reason for young people not complying was a breach of the requirement to report to a Bail Supervision and Support scheme.

Schemes found that the lack of suitable accommodation was a significant problem, and they made persistent efforts to address the issue.

You might care to reflect on some of these research findings, especially this last point.

Bail supervision and support applies to 10–17-year-olds. For those under 17, an alternative would be for the young person to be *accommodated* (section 23 Children and Young Persons Act 1969, see also Chapter 4), sometimes with conditions laid on the local authority such as not placing the young person with a named individual. This accommodation would most likely be foster care or some kind of residential provision, and not local authority 'secure accommodation' as such (only the local authority itself can apply specifically for a *secure accommodation order* and the grounds for these are quite specific – see Chapter 3).

If the court wishes to impose a *security requirement*, they may order this but only for 12–16-year-olds (section 97 Crime and Disorder Act 1998). In these cases the Youth Offending Team refers the matter directly to the Youth Justice Board which organises placements. For young men aged 15 or 16 courts also have the power to send them to secure training centres unless they are deemed to be *vulnerable* (in which case secure accommodation is to be preferred).

Seventeen-year-olds draw the short straw: the only option for them is custody if courts insist on secure detention before the case is heard. Not surprisingly, holding young people in custody before trial is quite controversial, given the high suicide rate of youth custody generally (Goldson, 2002). A number of campaigns have been mounted to challenge under-18s being held in custody at all. For example:

PRACTICE EXAMPLE 2

Campaign
Putting children in jail is indefensible

The Children Act 1989 exists to protect the most vulnerable young people in our society. So the Home Office's insistence that the Act should not apply to almost 3,000 children in prison or on remand was always morally wrong. A landmark court judgment confirms that the Home Secretary's position was also wrong in law (reference to R (on the application of the Howard League for Penal Reform) v Secretary of State for the Home Department and another [2002] All ER (D) 465 declaring that the Children Act 1989 did apply to youth custody institutions).

... The Howard League, the Children's Society and the coalition of children's charities which brought the case deserve Mr Justice Munby's commendation for bringing to public attention matters which ought to shock the conscience of every citizen. The 75-page judgment sets out in stark detail how placing children with chaotic and troubled backgrounds in a prison service designed for adult offenders exacerbates the worst of their lives to date. The high levels of bullying, of mental health problems, of self-harm and attempted suicide are, tragically, all too predictable...

Admitting that child prisoners have statutory and human rights may finally lead to the recognition that prison is no place for children.
(*The Observer*, Leader, 1 December 2002)

Dealing with first offenders

More accurately this section should perhaps be entitled 'first time offenders' or even 'first time in court offenders'. For, as has been explained, offences may have already resulted in a reprimand or some other action by the police or Youth Offending Team.

The Powers of Criminal Courts (Sentencing) Act 2000 requires the Youth Court to make a *referral order* on first time offenders who plead guilty. The Criminal Justice Act 2003 (section 324 and Schedule 34) allows a parenting order (see discussion in case study 2 above) to run alongside a referral order where this is appropriate. The referral order system was established by the Youth Justice and Criminal Evidence Act 1999 and implemented nationwide in 2002. This diverts the offender from the court to a youth offender panel which consists of one Youth Offending Team member and two other people drawn from the community, usually volunteers. This panel should negotiate a contract which lasts for as long as is specified by the court – but not less than three months and no more than 12. The panel is less formal than the court and aims to discuss in-depth with the offender and their family why they are in trouble and what steps can be taken to put right what they did wrong and to prevent further offences. In this process social worker involvement is important in terms of assessment and putting into effect the panel's decision, but the professional role remains advisory and Youth Offending Team members do not participate in decision-making. There would normally be a minimum of three meetings. The involvement of the victim, if there is one, is expected although whether the victim actually attends the panel is of course entirely a matter for them. Reparation is a key consideration and the referral panel system is based on the principles of restorative justice although not without its critics (see Further Reading and References).

Failure to co-operate with the Youth Offender Panel may mean that the matter is referred back to the Youth Court. The Youth Court then has powers to revoke the order if they wish and sentence the young person for the original offence.

After the first offence

If the young person admits the offence, or is found guilty, the court will request a pre-sentence report before deciding what sentence to impose. If they intend to consider only one particular sentence they may ask for a *specific sentence report* which follows the same format – this procedure is sometimes used for Action Plan Orders or Reparation Orders.

National Standards issued by the Youth Justice Board currently expect the reports to be submitted within three weeks (two for a persistent young offender). The assessment uses a common assessment tool (ASSET, national assessment guidelines, Youth Justice Board, see website listed at the end of the chapter) and advises the court about the young person's offending behaviour and action that can be taken to reduce re-offending. The key part of the reports makes a proposal regarding the sentence, or alternatively indicates which sentences would not be suitable. The final decision obviously rests with the court.

CASE STUDY

> *Damien aged 17 borrowed his mate's moped and rode it on a public road despite the fact that he knew he had no insurance. He had an accident on his fateful journey and damaged both the bike and a neighbour's car. This is his second bike-related offence.*

There would be a number of options for the Youth Court to consider in Damien's case. An absolute discharge, which effectively means no penalty and is used for very minor offences would clearly not be appropriate. Unless Damien has already received a final warning or is in breach of an anti-social behaviour order (section 66(4) Crime and Disorder Act 1998) the court could make a conditional discharge which simply means that if the offence is committed again within a fixed period of time (up to three years) the offender will be re-sentenced for the current offence as well as being punished for the new offence. A fine may be imposed – probably a hefty fine in this case as driving without insurance is regarded as a serious offence because of the potential consequences. Fines may be imposed on the parent or young person. Compensation for the damage may be awarded, here presumably for the damage to the neighbour's car, which the offender pays as a penalty. Probably not appropriate in this case, in some circumstances the court may make a reparation order. Exactly what this comprises is determined by the court on the advice of the social worker or Youth Offending Team member, but may not exceed 24 hours and must be completed within three months of making the order (section 74 Powers of Criminal Court (Sentencing) Act 2000).

ACTIVITY 6.1

Answer the following questions:

- *In what kinds of circumstances do you think a reparation order would be appropriate?*

- *What kinds of things could be done by means of reparation?*

The answer to the first question is for any kind of offence where there is clearly a victim, and where doing something, rather than paying something, seems an appropriate way of making it up to the victim. Appropriate activities might include gardening or household chores, decorating, repair work or anything that is going to be of clear tangible benefit to the victim, but obviously not something that would be exploitative. There are plainly some circumstances where reparation would not be appropriate: for example, where the victim cannot tolerate coming face-to-face with the offender.

Youth community orders and community sentences

CASE STUDY

Tom, aged 15, has committed his third offence of taking and driving away. As he is under age, he is charged with the associated offences of driving while disqualified through age and without insurance.

The orders that we have been discussing so far do not require a preliminary assessment of seriousness. However, we are now moving up the scale and in this section consider *community sentences* which apply where offences are *serious enough* to merit them (Criminal Justice Act 1991; Criminal Justice Act 2003).

Youth community orders as defined by the Powers of Criminal Court (Sentencing) Act 2000 comprise:

- attendance centre orders (section 163);

- action plan orders (section 69);

- curfew orders (section 163);

- supervision orders (section 63);

- exclusion orders (section 40A).

Community sentences as defined by the Criminal Justice and Court Services Act 2000 include:

- community rehabilitation orders;

- community punishment orders;

- community punishment and rehabilitation orders.

The last three community sentences apply only to offenders aged 16 or 17 years and are in effect what many people still call probation orders, community service orders and combination orders. The community punishment order involves offenders spending six to eight hours a week working on a community project for a total of between 40 and 240 hours. The Criminal Justice Act 2003 abolished the equivalent orders for adults.

Attendance centre orders are traditionally meant to deprive offenders of a short period of their liberty, quite often coinciding with football matches. Attendance at the centre, which can be operated by the police or Youth Offending Teams, consists of two- to three-hour long sessions on a weekly basis. Maximum total attendance is 24 hours for 10–15-year-olds and 36 hours for 16- and 17-year-olds.

These orders may be combined with an Action Plan Order which is more flexible, being designed to address the particular offender's needs. For example the plan may include a requirement to attend a training session of some kind, prohibitions on going to specific places, an order to engage in a programme of skills development, or to make some kind of reparation. Social workers have a key role in advising courts as to what should be included, and courts have the option of reviewing progress not more than 21 days after the order is made in order to ensure that it is working.

A more specific order, intended to prevent offending, is a Curfew Order which can stand on its own or be combined with other orders. This requires the offender to stay in certain places, a requirement that can be enforced by electronic monitoring ('tagging'). The order lasts for a maximum of six months for 16–17-year-olds (three months for under 16s) and can apply to periods of between two and twelve hours per day.

Supervision orders provide for direct involvement of a social worker as supervisor and adviser to the young offender and their family. Supervision consists of home visits or the young offender reporting to the Youth Offending Team's office, with the frequency of visits laid down by the Youth Justice Board's National Standards. Supervision orders are intended to address directly the welfare needs insomuch as they are relevant to the offending behaviour, and to this end there can be included certain kinds of requirements. These can include attendance at particular places, reparation, involvement in training or education, residence with a specified person, receiving medical treatment, desisting from certain activities and even being accommodated by the local authority for up to six months.

Youth Justice Next Steps (Home Office, 2003) proposed expanding Action Plan Orders with powers to impose up to three interventions from a broader comprehensive menu which includes all of the measures listed above. It was proposed that orders be made for a period of up to 24 months.

Custody

First of all it may not be the Youth Court that hears his case since, if his offence was committed with an adult, the magistrates court would have to consider where the case should be heard. There are a number of options but it is never possible for an adult to be tried in Youth Courts, so one outcome may be that the young person is tried in an adult court. Nevertheless the principle is that the young person's case should be remitted to the Youth Court whenever possible.

In this case Neil can consider himself very fortunate since if he were an adult and convicted of a third offence of burglary, he would automatically receive a sentence of three years' imprisonment (section 4 Crime (Sentences) Act 1997). As it is, he is at serious risk of receiving a custodial sentence. The Criminal Justice Act 1991 requires courts to decide that such an offence is so serious that only a custodial sentence is appropriate and this is highly likely in this case.

For young people the primary custodial sentence is the Detention and Training Order, for which the minimum age is 12. These orders can only be passed on 12- to 14-year-olds where they are deemed to be persistent young offenders. Detention and training are intended to run together in the sense that shortly after admission to custody a planning meeting is held. This involves the Youth Offending Team as well as the offender, parents and custodial establishment. Supervision of the training elements then continues in the community, once the offender has served half the period of the order in custody. The orders can be made for specific periods of four, six, eight, ten, 12, 18 or 24 months (Crime and Disorder Act 1998).

For the most serious cases of all, special provision is now made through the Powers of Criminal Courts (Sentencing) Act 2000. Young people who commit murder are detained *at Her Majesty's pleasure* (Section 90) meaning for at least a minimum period and then only when the parole board says they can be discharged into the community (under licence). For other *grave* offences, for which an adult could be sent to prison for 14 years or more, the young offender can be detained up to a maximum period laid down for that offence (Section 91). In both cases the young person will be held in a secure unit at the age of 15, being transferred at that age to a Young Offender Institution and then to an adult prison at the age of 18. This is the procedure (under previous legislation) that applied to the young men convicted of the murder of Jamie Bulger in 1993.

Special kinds of orders

Just to complete the picture there are five other kinds of orders that can be made, some of which will apply to young offenders very occasionally.

First, people with serious drug dependency problems can be made subject to a drug treatment and testing order, providing they consent. It effectively substitutes residential or community drug addiction treatment for a custodial or community sentence, and the order lasts between six months and three years.

Second, a hospital order applies to people who are mentally ill or have another form of mental disorder and where the circumstances warrant it (Chapter 5 made reference to the definitions of mental disorder). There is no lower age limit for most disorders so, potentially, hospital orders could apply to a young offender. Hence social workers working in the field of mental health and youth justice would need to know more about this provision and how it relates to supervision in the community after discharge (comprehensively covered in Jones, 2006).

Third, parents of young offenders can be bound over to ensure they comply with community sentences and in order to prevent further offences. Binding over means that parents undertake to exercise *proper care and control* and can be required to pay up to £1,000 if there are further offences or failure to comply with the requirements of the community sentences (section 150 Powers of Criminal Court (Sentencing) Act 2000).

Fourth, Intensive Supervision and Surveillance Programmes use combinations of the various powers detailed above in the Crime and Disorder Act 1998, the Powers of Criminal Court (Sentencing) Act 2000 and the Criminal Justice and Courts Services Act 2000 and are targeted at persistent young offenders or those who commit particularly serious crimes. They offer programmes of intensive supervision usually for six months with 24-hour monitoring. This might include electronic tagging, combined with bail supervision and support, community supervision and Detention and Training orders. There are currently 81 schemes with programmes available to Youth Offending Teams throughout England and Wales (see Youth Justice Board website at the end of this chapter).

Finally there is a sex offender order which is preventative in that it is not a penalty, but can be applied for through the civil courts where there is reasonable cause to believe that someone is acting suspiciously towards children (sections 2–4 Crime and Disorder Act 1998). Application for the order and its implementation is primarily a police matter, but clearly social workers and teachers ought to be aware of this as a potential way of protecting children in schools and organised activities. It may be worth noting in passing that young people who are convicted of certain sexual offences are, like adults, obliged to have their names entered on the sex offenders register, although for half the period of time for which the adult is required to register (section 82 Sexual Offences Act 2003). This register, established by the Sex Offenders Act 1997, is maintained by the police and includes basic information such as name, date of birth and address. Parents of young sex offenders are required to ensure that the offender registers and reports as required (section 89 Sexual Offences Act 2003).

Experiencing the youth justice system

In this section we would like you to find out about the experience of users of the youth justice system. Here we include victims of crime as well as those who commit offences and are therefore on the 'receiving end' of youth justice.

ACTIVITY 6.2

Find out what you can about one of the following topics:

- *the experience of young people as victims of crime; or*

- *young offenders' views of their own experience of youth justice.*

It is up to you to decide how to set about this task, but if you need help there are some suggestions in the Exercise Answers, p148.

It is also up to you to decide how long you want to spend on this exercise. You may even wish to develop it into a mini project if this fits in with the requirements of your social work programme.

Apart from developing your research skills, the purpose of the exercise was to get you in touch with the views, reactions and feelings of people who experience the youth justice system. If you tackled the question on victims, you will no doubt have discovered that little attention, relatively speaking, has been paid to the experience of young people as victims of crime. It sometimes comes as a surprise to older people to discover that young people are disproportionately more likely to be the victims of crime. If you attempted the question on young offenders' experiences, you will have encountered a range of responses, with very varied degrees of acceptance of personal responsibility for offences committed.

On the basis of this research, you may care to consider the implications for practice. Should more attention be paid to the needs of victims of crime, especially younger victims? Should court sentencing pay greater attention to individual differences amongst offenders? What exactly should the role of the social worker be in the youth justice system and how should they balance the needs of victims and offenders?

C H A P T E R   S U M M A R Y

In this chapter, we used a variety of case studies to explain the role of the social worker in the youth justice system. We started with the prevention of crime, the central role of local authorities in running multi-professional Youth Offending Teams, and anti-social behaviour orders as preventative measures. We then went on to look at what happens when an alleged offender is arrested and bailed or detained. This led to a consideration of the first stage of court proceedings when an offender receives their first conviction. We then proceeded through the tariffs for subsequent offences, looking at the various kinds of community sentences and custody, with additional reference to certain kinds of special orders available in particular circumstances. We concluded with a very small-scale research assignment that asked you to investigate either the experience of young people as victims of crime or the experience of young offenders who have experienced the youth justice system at first hand.

Finally, if you decide to work in this area, you will need to keep very alert to new developments as this is one area of social work where there is a great deal of political interest and where governments are always seeking to make an impact.

For the background to youth justice and practice issues not covered here it would be useful to look at the following:

Dugmore, P, Pickford, J and Angus, S (2006) Youth Justice and Social Work. Exeter: Learning Matters.

Goldson, B and Muncie, J (2006) Youth Crime and Justice. London: Sage.

Stephenson, M, Giller, H and Brown, S (2007) Effective Practice in Youth Justice. Cullompton: Willan.

Criminal Justice website: **www.cjsonline.org**

Home Office: **www.homeoffice.gov.uk/**

Home Office Youth Justice and Children unit documents: **www.homeoffice.gov.uk/about-us/organ isation/directorate-search/noms/olsp/jou/version=1**

Youth Justice Board: **www.yjb.gov.uk/en-gb/**

For further information on the Children's Society work in youth justice see: **www.childrenssociety. org.uk**

Chapter 7
Ending up in court

Introduction

This chapter applies the law in a very practical way by looking at what happens when cases end up in court.

The comparatively lengthy list of standards above indicates how central court working is to some aspects of social work. Social work often involves making major decisions that can have far-reaching consequences for families. It is only right and proper that there should be a strong measure of public accountability – public in this case meaning through the system of public law and procedures authorised by Parliament, not through the press and publicity as such.

Why is the court so important as a forum for decision-making in social work?

Have a go at answering this question yourself.

Working on your own or in conjunction with other students or colleagues, what reasons can you suggest as to why it is important for social workers to be accountable to the court? List as many reasons as you can in about ten minutes.

Here are some suggestions; this list is by no means exhaustive and you may have suggested other equally valid reasons not listed here.

- The courts are independent of social services departments, children's services authorities and other agencies that employ social workers.

- This offers service users a means of challenging decisions social workers make, and offers social workers an independent view on the appropriateness of their plans.

- Courts bring everything out into the open, and all information has to be shared. This may offer people opportunities to obtain information which they think is important.

- Courts implement the law, and social workers must operate within the law. If necessary, courts can tell social workers that what they are doing is not legally justifiable.

- People are represented in court through solicitors or barristers, and this gives them an opportunity for advocacy through which assessments, plans and decisions can be tested or challenged.

- As a matter of principle, it seems appropriate that major life-changing decisions ought to be confirmed by a credible body that offers independent scrutiny.

- Important decisions about people's lives are shared with other professionals (lawyers) and validated or confirmed by an independent body that only concerns itself with what is lawful and verifiable.

- Courts balance the rights of individuals against the rights of the state, and can also distinguish between the rights and interests of parents as against the rights and interests of children where these differ. The earlier discussion in Chapter 1 concerning the Cleveland Report (DHSS, 1988) is obviously relevant here.

When are social workers likely to end up in court?

As a social worker, when might you be required to attend court in a professional capacity?

Tom, aged 15, has committed his third offence of taking and driving away. As he is under age, he is charged with the associated offences of driving while disqualified through age and without insurance.

CASE STUDY

Mandy (7) and Melissa (5) have been left in their house alone at night on a number of occasions, while parents have been out visiting friends who are known to be drug users. Attempts to help parents understand how dangerous this is have proved fruitless, to the extent that the local authority now believes its only recourse is to institute care proceedings and ask for a supervision order on both girls.

There are two important areas of social work where practitioners regularly give evidence in court. The first is in relation to youth justice, and this will apply to Tom's case. As we saw in Chapter 6, the general practice is for social workers to combine with professionals from other disciplines in order to form multidisciplinary teams working in the youth justice field. Each member of the team has particular responsibilities, but when it comes to advising courts about possible sentencing outcomes, and reporting to courts on the progress of supervision of young offenders, all members of the team share this responsibility. On occasion, this will include not only writing reports for the court, but also appearing in them. The second area of work is children and families, specifically in cases where care proceedings are instituted, as in the case of Mandy and Melissa. Chapter 4 introduced the grounds for instituting care proceedings, laying emphasis on the notion of *significant harm* (Section 31 Children Act 1989). Significant harm has to be proved in court and to the court's satisfaction. It is in the court that magistrates or judges need to be persuaded of the necessity of making an order, and are advised about the kind of order necessary to secure the best possible future for the child.

There are other instances where courts sometimes hear from social workers. In matters of domestic violence proceedings under the Family Law Act 1996 (as augmented by the Domestic Violence, Crime and Victims Act 2004), it is possible that social workers might be asked to give evidence in the county court. In criminal cases, social workers have the same responsibilities as every other citizen to give evidence where they have witnessed a crime, but additionally social workers may sometimes be asked to be present when certain people are interviewed at police stations. This is called acting as an *appropriate adult* (section 66 Code of Practice Police and Criminal Evidence Act 1984). This requires the police to have someone present when young people (under 17) or people with mental health problems or learning difficulties are interviewed, although it may be worth noting that this does not necessarily have to be a social worker – in many cases it would be parents or another family member (NACRO, 2003b; Brammer, 2007: pp398–399, 567–568). Specialist and non-specialist social workers are sometimes asked to furnish reports to Mental Health Review Tribunals and attend their hearings. These reports outline the social circumstances of the patient and the facilities available in the community to offer rehabilitation and supervision if the patient is discharged from hospital. Given the important role of the tribunal in determining whether people who have been compulsorily detained in psychiatric hospitals should be discharged, it is important for such social workers to understand their precise task. In very rare cases, the High Court may be called upon to adjudicate where a service user alleges that the local authority has acted inappropriately by not interpreting the law correctly. It is just possible that social workers might be called upon to give evidence in such cases (see Chapter 2 for general rights of redress and an overview of how social work agencies are held accountable more widely).

In the first part of this chapter, we will be addressing some of the fears, anxieties and mis-apprehensions that social workers often share about appearing in court. The aim here is to take away some of the mythology about giving evidence. Courts need not be a stressful experience if practitioners are aware of basic procedures, the principles of giving evidence, and develop a clear idea about what courts expect of them. The second part of the chapter therefore offers an overview of what goes on in courts, distinguishing the different roles people play in Youth Courts, based on criminal law, and Family Proceedings Courts, based on civil law (for explanation of the differences between criminal and civil law see Chapter 1). This part of the chapter addresses the specific expectations of the social worker in these courts, with specific references to pre-sentence reports (Youth Court) and statement preparation (Family Proceedings Court). Then follows a section devoted to service users' perspectives, and research and policy debates about court proceedings. This enables the chapter to conclude with reflections on good practice that includes preparing service users for court, acting professionally in court and working in a way that incorporates key social work values.

Appearing in court can be fun

It may seem incredible, but that is the view of some practitioners! To them court is an enjoyable experience because it is challenging: it is good to have one's competence and knowledge tested out, and helps to keep the practitioner focused. It compels them to think clearly about the case and is therefore a stimulating intellectual exercise. Furthermore, from a practice point of view it is invaluable in clarifying issues that are of concern: young people cannot deny being in difficulties if they are convicted of an offence by a court, parents cannot deny family problems if a court determines that their child is being *significantly harmed*. Thus court is a cathartic experience: it liberates people to concentrate on the real issues.

For those who are not initially quite so enthusiastic, it is important to remember that appearing in court need not be anxiety provoking. Courts are not set up to catch people out; yet their role is crucial in terms of public accountability for social work. It is in a court that the social worker sometimes has to justify their actions, and certainly has to justify the outcomes of an assessment where it is intended to propose a specific course of action that is opposed by others. The primary purpose of the court is to test the evidence through which people have drawn certain conclusions. If the children's services authority has concluded that the best interests of the child will be served by placing them with foster carers, and this move is opposed by the parents, it is only right and proper that the parents should have some way of having that conclusion critically scrutinised, or in legal jargon, *cross-examined*. The public needs to be assured that the proposed way of dealing with young offenders is one which minimises the chances of the young person committing a further offence. The sentence should also be justified in terms of being *proportionate* to the seriousness of the offence.

How confident do you feel about appearing in court and giving evidence? The following activity asks you to explore your feelings about giving evidence in a court as a witness. It does not matter for the purpose of the exercise whether you imagine this to be a court set up to hear a criminal case, such as the Youth Court, or one that is concerned with civil matters such as care proceedings.

ACTIVITY 7.2

Take a blank sheet of paper and draw a line down the middle so that you have two columns.

Fears about court	Impressions I would like to convey

You may like to do this exercise with someone else, working as a pair, or even in a group. Start with the left-hand column and think of how you would feel if someone told you that tomorrow morning you have to go to court to give evidence. Try to be as honest as you can and also try to be as specific as you can. It is important to complete the left-hand column before starting on the positives on the right-hand side. After spending about ten minutes or so on the fears and apprehensions, move on to the impressions you would most like to convey. Do spend the same amount of time on the right-hand column. It may be more difficult to list the impressions you would like to convey, but it will certainly repay you to do so.

Even the most experienced practitioners have some nervousness about appearing in court. Some of the most common fears and anxieties are:

- fear of the unknown: ignorance of the 'ground rules', not knowing when to do what;

- the physical symptoms of nervousness;

- being afraid that you will forget something vital, such as the case summary;

- worrying that you will be 'tricked' into saying something you don't mean, or will fall into a 'clever' lawyer's trap;

- believing that you are going to make a complete fool of yourself by a combination of all of the above;

- consequently being left feeling that not only have you let yourself down, you have also betrayed the confidence of the child, family or young person you were meant to be helping.

It is possible to avert most of these fears through careful preparation, prediction of what will happen, practising giving evidence and, above all, by adopting a professional approach.

Preparation

If court procedure really is new to you, try to spend a day observing what goes on in courts. Magistrates courts in most large towns or cities sit almost daily, and the public are allowed to attend most proceedings. It may be worth a preliminary check with the clerk of the court's office if you are not sure when courts sit, or which will be open to the public. Not all cases are equally interesting, but the purpose of the exercise is for you to see what happens when people are asked to give evidence. Whilst there are some minor differences between courts, general procedures are similar in all courts and at all levels (for an explanation of different kinds of courts see below).

In all cases, it is important to know the facts about the case and to know how to distinguish between facts, opinion and interpretation. Have the papers in order so the report or case records can be referred to: large documents can be divided into sections that are clearly identifiable. Being familiar with research findings that support the opinions or recommendations offered to the court is to be applauded. Evidence-based practice is more persuasive to courts than opinions simply based on intuition or emotions.

Practice

Go through the evidence in advance, preferably with a colleague who can pick up on points that appear to be unclear or inconsistent. Familiarise yourself with the case to the extent that you are confident about it, that you really know what information is relevant for the court in its deliberations. As a social worker in care proceedings, you will be attending court in a professional capacity with access to the support and guidance of lawyers who are either employed by the same authority as yourself, or else contracted to provide legal services to your employer. It is therefore highly advisable to contact this lawyer in advance and to run through basic procedures with them. Do not hesitate to explain that this is your first time in court if that is the case.

If nervousness and apprehension are problems, try using relaxation techniques. It really does not matter what kind as long as they work for you.

Prediction

It is usually possible to anticipate the kind of questions courts are going to ask. It is rare that people are going to try playing tricks on the social worker by throwing in questions that could not be anticipated. It is nearly always possible to predict the areas in which the court is likely to be interested: what would you ask if you were the magistrate or the judge? What are the points at which the service user or family disagree with the social work professionals? In what ways do the grandparents' views, for example, differ from the views of the parents or indeed from those of the social work professionals? Bear in mind, too, the legal issues which the court is bound to consider. In criminal cases the court must weigh up the seriousness of the offence. In care proceedings cases, the court is bound to enquire about the *welfare checklist* (section 1 Children Act 1989; see Chapter 4) and will also be aware of the need not to be discriminatory. For example, regulations require considerations of race, culture and religion to be incorporated into care plans. It is most likely therefore that courts will ask questions about the care plan and specifically about this aspect.

Professionalism

Professionalism refers to very practical issues such as observing the dress code and ensuring that one's personal appearance accords the court with the respect it thinks it deserves. Dressing appropriately for court is very important since it demonstrates respect, and courts, rightly or wrongly, regard dress that is too casual as an indication that the person is too casual. More importantly, it risks prejudicing the court against the social worker's case and thereby potentially does the child or young person a disservice.

Witnesses should assume that they will be standing to give evidence unless the court makes it clear that people will be sitting throughout, as is now general practice in magistrates' family proceedings courts, or invites the witness to sit. Witnesses should address the 'bench' of magistrates or the judge, not the person who actually asks the question. This is much more difficult than it sounds, for it is natural to look at the person posing questions. One way of overcoming this is to turn one's feet towards the bench or magistrates and in that way make addressing the bench or judge more natural.

When answering questions it is important to speak clearly and concisely, but equally important not to rush into an answer. There is no obligation to answer questions quickly, but there is a duty to answer questions honestly. If, for example, there is a conflict of opinion, it is definitely not a good idea to try to cover this up. Above all, evidence should be presented using plain English avoiding the temptation to use jargon. Social work is not exempt from jargon, all professions have their own specific language, but in this context jargon is particularly deplorable since it is not only disrespectful to the court but, more importantly, disempowers families and thereby stops them participating fully in the proceedings.

The final aspect of professionalism is the most important: never take it personally. By this is meant that there should never be a degree of personal and emotional investment or involvement in the case to the extent that the outcome matters if it doesn't go 'your' way. In the 1960s there was a television series concerning a lawyer called Perry Mason who tirelessly, every week, won every single case while his opponent equally tirelessly lost every case. Life is not like that. No lawyer expects to 'win' every case and no social worker should expect every court to go along precisely with their view. If courts simply rubber stamped social work decision-making, there would simply be no point having a court system and the consequences for service users would be all too obvious. It is much healthier for social workers to be challenged regularly, for assessments to be scrutinised and for decisions to be tested robustly in the court setting. For social workers this means inevitably that decisions will not always go 'their' way.

Who's who in the court system?

What can you expect to find when a court is sitting? What roles do the professionals play? Here there are some differences between the different kinds of court.

Youth Court

A Practice Direction issued by the Lord Chief Justice (Trial of Children and Young Persons in the Crown Court, February 2000) sets out some principles by which criminal courts should organise procedures and settings for cases involving under 18-year-olds. These include:

All possible steps should be taken to assist the young defendant to understand and participate in the proceedings (paragraph 3)

The trial should, if practicable, be held in a courtroom in which all the participants are on the same or almost the same level (paragraph 9)

A young defendant should normally, if he wishes, be free to sit with members of his family or others in a place which permits easy, informal communication with his legal representatives and others ... (paragraph 11)

Practice direction (criminal: consolidated) (2002) 3 All ER 904: 39.3, 39.9, 39.10

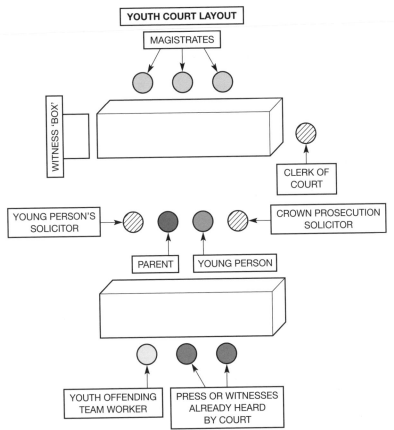

Note: ⊘ legally qualified personnel. Court sits on one level but is stricter on procedure than Family Proceedings Court. People give evidence formally. Young people can choose whether to sit with parent, solicitor, YOT worker or another relative. There may be local variations to this pattern. Not all courts are the same.

Family Proceedings Court

Informality is particularly important in family proceedings and it is now virtually standard practice for people to remain seated when they address the magistrates. However, in some courts it is still customary for witnesses to stand while they present their evidence. It is also expected that parents will sit next to their advocate, whilst children do not normally attend court. It is assumed that the kind of evidence brought before the court is unsuitable for children to hear and, except in very rare instances, the court will appoint a guardian who speaks for the child and can instruct a solicitor or barrister to advocate for the child's point of view in court.

In general witnesses should wait outside the court before they are called. This is to prevent them hearing evidence from other witnesses, although sometimes professional witnesses are allowed to stay throughout the whole hearing. Professional witnesses are expected to have written records and documents available to them for reference when giving evidence, but should not normally refer to them without permission of the court. Counsel representing the local authority might ask permission before the social worker presents their evidence (technically the 'examination-in-chief'). Or the social worker may simply ask before opening the file: *May I refer to my notes?*

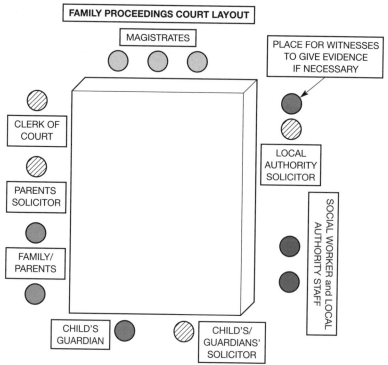

Note: ⊘ = legally qualified personnel.
Court sits on one level around a table. People address the court and give evidence seated, but there may be local differences in custom and practice. Not all courts are the same.

County Court

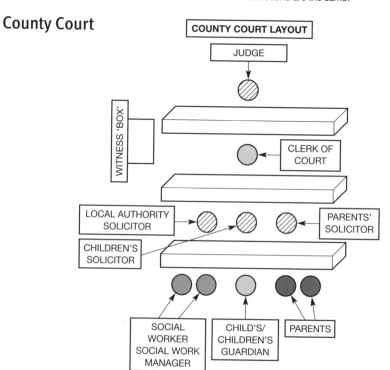

Note: ⊘ legally qualified personnel. Court is on different levels with judge higher than everyone else. Procedure more formal then other courts. People give evidence formally and legal personnel may be wearing robes and gowns. There may be local variations to this pattern. Not all courts are the same.

It will be seen from this diagram that courts with judges tend to have a more formal arrangement, and this is reflected in their procedures. Witnesses invariably stand through-out their evidence. Likewise advocates stand to address the judge and rules of procedure, such as administration of the oath or affirmation, are strictly enforced.

Magistrates and judges

Magistrates are lay people, appointed from the local community, who undergo additional training for a job that is essentially unpaid. There are some specific provisions and qualifi-cations applicable to those appointed to Youth Courts or Family Proceedings Courts. A bench of magistrates is so called because it consists of three (usually) magistrates sitting in a row, although these days not actually on a bench! It is customary for only one magis-trate, the chair, to speak for the bench. Very occasionally there will be one magistrate sitting alone – for example, in criminal cases in very busy areas where the magistrate is legally qualified and full-time and sits as a District Judge (Magistrates Court). Magistrates are usually addressed as *Sir* or *Madam* or, collectively, as *Your Worships*.

Judges are experienced barristers (normally) or solicitors (occasionally) who hear the more serious criminal cases or the more complex family proceedings cases. Judges sit alone. In family proceedings cases, judges will have been chosen for their experience in cases involving children and families, and it is the expectation that at the county court level judges will deal with the more difficult care proceedings cases. In a High Court, judges will deal with appeals from the magistrates' Family Proceedings Courts as well as deciding on the really complex cases, such as those cases which involve children living in different countries or highly contested adoption cases. At the very highest level of the court structure, the Appeal Courts, judges do sometimes hear cases together making a panel of three or five judges. There are some variations as to how judges are addressed depending on their status. Generally county court judges are referred to as *Your Honour* but in higher courts judges may be *My Lord* or *My Lady* – ask legal representatives if unsure.

The following diagram shows the relationship of the courts to each other in a form of hierarchy.

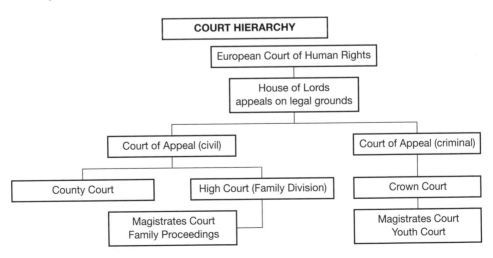

Barristers and solicitors (advocates)

The legal profession is divided into two branches. Barristers, sometimes referred to as 'counsel', are regarded as specialists in advocacy; that is, in presenting cases and speaking on their client's behalf. Solicitors may also be advocates but generally will deal with a wider range of cases than barristers. Barristers cannot take 'instructions' direct from their clients, but usually operate through an 'instructing' solicitor. There are certain rules regarding courts in which solicitors and barristers may appear with the general principle being that only barristers have the right of 'audience' in the very highest courts.

Court clerks and other court officials

As magistrates are lay people they often need the assistance of someone legally qualified, their clerk. There are restrictions on the powers of magistrates and in some cases they are obliged to send (remit) cases to higher courts. The clerk's job is to organise the court and supervise the administration of justice, being responsible for collecting fines, allocating cases, ensuring there are magistrates available and so on. In care proceedings cases, clerks will also chair the discussion of timetabling and make agreed orders regarding disclosure of documents and evidence ('directions hearings').

In County Courts and High Courts, since the judge is legally qualified, the clerk does not need to be so. Hence clerks in these cases are most often just that: people who take notes or look up calendars or reference books for the judge.

Ushers are the people who act as receptionists, call cases into court, show people where to go, administer the oath and generally ensure people are where they should be.

Police and Crown Prosecution Service

The police are not generally involved in family proceedings cases, unless there is a specific reason to call a police officer as a witness. Similarly, the police are not routinely involved in Youth Court cases unless required to give specific evidence since the case is conducted by the Crown Prosecution Service, who will employ a solicitor to present the case. The role of the Crown Prosecution Service is to sift the cases which have been investigated by the police so as to ensure that only those where prosecution is deemed appropriate are taken to court (for website address see end of chapter).

Guardians

Children's Guardians are social workers who specialise in court work with children in the Family Proceedings Courts, and are appointed to specific cases by the Child and Family Court Advisory and Support Service (CAFCASS: for website address see end of chapter). This body was set up by the Criminal Justice and Court Services Act 2000 (with special arrangements for Wales: See Sections 35–41 Children Act 2004) in order to offer a comprehensive child representation service to the courts (section 12 Children Act 1989). It took over responsibility from local authorities for the *guardian-ad-litem* service, and legislation and rules still refer in many cases to the *guardian-ad-litem* although the terminology has now changed. Children's Guardians must be independent of the local authority involved in the case, and it is their role to conduct an independent investigation on behalf of the court and to speak for the child. They instruct lawyers to act for the child so as to ensure that the child's perspective (and not just the parents') is conveyed to the court (section 41 Children Act 1989). Guardians have rights of access to local authority documents relating to children (section 42 Children Act 1989) and can call witnesses to court as well as giving independent advice and evidence to courts themselves.

Social workers

Social workers are regarded as professional witnesses, that is, people who are giving evidence by virtue of the position they hold and the role they play in a family's life as an adviser. Hence the role is unlike someone who gives evidence in a criminal case who happens to see a robbery or a road accident. Being a professional witness means the courts can and often do ask for that person's advice and opinion, and expect a professional witness to be able to support their conclusions by reference to research-based evidence as well as by reference to the facts of the case.

Social workers need to be aware that when they are giving evidence they are officers of the court, that is, their first duty is to the court, to tell all that they know and to answer all questions truthfully. There may, on rare occasions, be a conflict of views with their own managers, or with other social workers. The court is entitled to know that there is disagreement; one local authority advises its staff that honesty in these circumstances at least indicates the complexity of the case to the court. Whilst social workers are professionally accountable to their managers they cannot hide behind someone else's opinion as to what should happen in a particular case. They must present and support their own view. For further discussion of the general issue of accountability see Chapter 8.

Social workers in the Youth Court need to prepare pre-sentence reports in accordance with national guidelines issued by the Youth Justice Board (Youth Justice Board, 2004).

Social workers in family proceedings have a particular role in collating the background information for the court and putting this together as a chronology (list of events in date order) and statement. If this is all new to you, look under Further Reading at the end of this chapter for additional sources of advice.

Social workers can also be used as independent expert witnesses carrying out instructions for a lawyer. This may happen when someone wants the social work equivalent of a 'second opinion' and the social worker is then called to give evidence on their behalf. Nevertheless, in such situations it still remains the case that the social worker's obligations are to the court and they must give their honest professional opinion.

What happens in court?

How will the courts decide what to do in the cases of Tom Bates, accused of taking and driving away motor vehicles, and Mandy and Melissa Watson who are too young to be left to look after themselves (see previous case studies)?

Underlying principles that determine what happens in court

The court system is often described as adversarial. The use of this term implies almost continuously hostile conflict, which is rarely the case. Rather it is a technical term that refers to the system whereby the court itself cannot initiate proceedings, cannot call witnesses and cannot consider anything other than what is presented before it. It is for those bringing the cases, referred to as the *applicants*, to present to the court all the evidence they think they need to 'prove' their case. It is then for the *respondents* (formerly referred to as *defendants*) to present their side of the argument, often refuting or challenging the evidence presented by the applicants.

In criminal cases such as Tom's the applicant is always the Crown, hence the case would be referred to as R (for Regina) *v* (for versus) Bates. In civil cases (the differences between civil and criminal law were explained in Chapter 1) the surnames of applicants and respondents are used, or else the name of the local authority or organisation concerned. So in care proceedings it might be Anyshire County Council *v* Watson, or if it were a dispute between two parents, Watson *v* Watson.

Nevertheless one principle is common to both criminal and civil cases, namely that generally they all start in the Magistrates Courts (one exception is adoption cases which may start in the County Court). Here one would start in the Youth Court branch of the Magistrates Court, whilst the other would start in the Magistrates Family Proceedings Court. This rule applies even though it is intended that the case will be sent to other courts such as the Crown Court for criminal cases and County or High Court for civil cases.

Who starts the proceedings?

Criminal cases are initiated by the police referring the matter to the Crown Prosecution Service who have the ultimate responsibility in deciding whether or not to bring a case before the courts. Care proceedings cases are started by the applicant, usually the local authority, sending a form to the court. This contains some basic information concerning the grounds and is usually prepared by lawyers. In urgent cases, care proceedings begin with an Emergency Protection Order (section 44 Children Act 1989) which is immediately referred to the court who decide the next steps. Courts have the authority to adjourn cases for as many times as necessary, although there are rules regarding care proceedings and the duration of, for example, interim care orders (for information on these rules look at section 38 Children Act 1989 and the Family Proceedings Court (Children Act 1989) Rules 1991). However, serious concern has been expressed about delays in both criminal and civil cases and the Youth Court is a target for initiatives to reduce delays in offenders coming to court. Family Proceedings Courts operate under the statutory presumption that any delay *is likely to prejudice the welfare of the child* (section 1(2) Children Act 1989) so are charged with making directions, at what are know as *direction hearings*, about the timetabling and progress of cases through, for example, requiring certain documents to be produced by specific dates.

Given the adversarial system whereby one side presents evidence which can then be challenged by the other, the procedure is predictable in that the applicant presents all their evidence first before handing on to the respondents. By this is meant that the applicant calls all their witnesses first, but naturally each witness can be challenged (or technically cross-examined) by the 'other side'. The first stage of this evidence is called the *examination in chief* and there are strict rules about the ways in which lawyers can ask questions in this examination. When it comes to cross-examination, questioning can take a different form including asking what are known as leading questions (questions that imply an answer). Magistrates or judges have the right to ask questions if they wish. It is also possible to re-examine witnesses and occasionally to recall witnesses if an issue comes up which has not been foreseen and it is relevant for the courts to do so, but note there are custom and practice rules about this.

Privacy and confidentiality

Family proceedings by their very nature involve very personal information about a family being laid out before strangers – magistrates, court clerks, solicitors, social workers. It is essential in order to preserve privacy and confidentiality for the hearings to be held in private and so all hearings are held *in camera*. This means no one is allowed to attend unless they have a clear connection to the case which they can prove to the court's satisfaction if necessary; no public report can be made about the case so no newspaper can report Mandy and Melissa's case, although the Children Act 2004 (section 62) allows the possibility of courts publishing information in exceptional circumstances where there is a matter of general public interest.

By contrast, the media are entitled to attend the Youth Court and may report cases so long as the media do not identify those involved, so Tom's name won't appear in the papers, although the details of his offences might. Furthermore, the law prohibits the publication of any report or picture which might help reveal the name, address or school of the young person concerned, although it is possible for courts to lift these restrictions if it is in the public interest to do so – such as if the court thinks publicity will help stop them offending (section 49 Children and Young Persons Act 1933, as amended). Furthermore, reporting restrictions are automatically lifted if the Youth Court is considering the breach of an anti-social behaviour order (section 141 Serious Organised Crime and Police Act 2005).

Outcomes

The burden or onus of proof lies always with the person who initiates the proceedings. In Tom's case he is assumed innocent until proven guilty and the prosecution must prove to the court that he is. In Mandy and Melissa's case the local authority has to prove the grounds for care proceedings before the court can contemplate making an order.

The standard of proof is a technical term referring to the test by which the court is guided when it determines a case. The important distinction here is between criminal cases such as Tom's where the court must be convinced *beyond reasonable doubt* that the offender is guilty, whereas in civil cases it is necessary to prove this *on the balance of probabilities*, which is generally regarded as a less stringent test. So in care proceedings cases like Mandy and Melissa's it is the second test, the balance of probabilities, that applies.

Courts are required to give a decision in accordance with certain procedures. It is not general practice in criminal cases to explain decisions; they are simply announced. Occasionally, if there is an appeal, magistrates may be asked to provide some kind of explanation to the higher court. However, in family proceedings cases the court does have to give reasons for their conclusions and these need to be written down.

What does it feel like to go to court?

Earlier you were asked about your fears and apprehensions about appearing in court, but how does it feel to go through court as a service user?

Parental perspectives on care proceedings

Key findings of research carried out for the Department of Health as part of a major evaluation of the Children Act 1989.

RESEARCH SUMMARY

- *Parents often held very negative views of the child protection system, especially where court orders were sought on children who had already been accommodated on a voluntary basis.*

- *The services offered to families before they reached court were seen as inadequate and focused only on the child's needs rather than on those of the parents.*

- *Few parents felt they had participated in decision-making even when they had attended case conferences.*

- *Most parents were ill-prepared for court proceedings and felt marginalised and unsupported. Many found the court experience intimidating and confusing.*

- *The majority of solicitors representing parents did not have specific expertise in this area of law.*

- *Little support was available for parents after care proceedings had ended, whether or not they retained their child.*

- *Despite the generally negative views held by parents, there was potential for improving their experience of the court process.*

(Freeman and Hunt, 1998)

So much for the general scene, but how does it feel at a personal level? The following is a very articulate personal account from a father whose care case eventually ended up in the High Court.

Facing deportation

The main entrance hall of the Royal Courts of Justice is one of those buildings designed, it seems, to make one feel humble. Once through the doorway the roof soars high, footsteps echo from the tiled floor, the benches and arched roof imply that this is a sacred place. The link between justice and divinity is direct and potent. Is this a court or a cathedral? Has one come to stand before a human judge, or to meet one's maker?...

It did become clear throughout the process that professionals on the whole have very circumscribed choices, and are likely to be very vulnerable themselves if they are seen to get something wrong. The danger here is the potential for professionals becoming interested only in the evidence that will support their view .... Suddenly, a level of informality and openness I had experienced was ended. I became acutely aware of sources of power available to agencies when the accessibility, informality and the possibility of influence vanished.

It was as if I had been semi-hypnotised, watching this machinery working over several years, then awoken suddenly to find myself in its jaws.
(Tosey, 2000, p16)

Children's perspectives on care proceedings

The next extract summarises some research that centred on children's experiences of care proceedings. When reading this, remember that children do not normally attend court (Family Proceedings Court (Children Act 1989) Rules 1991), so the research was especially interested in what happened when children expressed a wish to do so.

RESEARCH SUMMARY

Thirty-five children reported that they were not consulted about whether they wished to attend court... The nine children who were asked all chose to attend. Only one attended the final hearing. She commented that, despite having prior agreement to sit in on the proceedings, when the day arrived she could not bring herself to go any further than the waiting room. The others either attended directions hearings or visited the court building. One child spoke directly with the judge in his chambers...

Seventeen of the children interviewed said they would like to have attended court, some because they wished for the opportunity to talk directly with the judiciary, others because they wanted to be more involved. They gave as their reasons, I wanted to see the judges. I don't even know what they look like. I wanted to be there, not in school when they were deciding and if my mum was upset I could tell her I'll still be seeing you *(boy, age 8).* I would like to see the judge and talk to him and I'll ask him if I can go home to my mum *(girl, age 9).* I would like to go to the court so I could say my own words *(girl age 8).* I would like to see it because I have never been before and everyone else went when I had to go to school *(girl age 9).*
(Ruegger, 2001, pp40–41)

Being on the receiving end of the justice system

Finally, what are the issues for people who experience the criminal justice court system at first hand? Once you are in practice as a social worker, there will be no shortage of people who can comment on this! However, in order to present a broader picture it may be useful at this stage to consider the conclusions drawn by the government in *Justice for all* (Home Office, 2002b) on the basis of research and consultation. This White Paper, which focused on the operation of the criminal justice system overall, had this to say about the criminal justice court system and its responsiveness to its service users:

7.18 .... Although it helps protect the rights of participants for courts to convey a sense of authority, we recognise that some aspects, such as formal dress, technical or old-fashioned language and obscure procedures, can make courts appear intimidating and inaccessible to many people.

7.19 We are looking at ways to make the courts, including Youth Courts, more accessible and less intimidating to the communities they serve. This is not window-dressing, but part of a much wider process of modernisation which extends to listing arrangements, use of information technology, proper treatment of victims and witnesses, and the provision of better information to the public...

7.21 More generally, we are committed to making courts more welcoming places for people to attend. As part of this, we will explore whether there are appropriate alternatives to the formal courtroom for the hearing of some cases, particularly those involving young and vulnerable victims, witnesses and defendants. Advantages could include a more accessible and less forbidding court process and reduced travel time. In developing these ideas, we will take account of the existing plans for civil and family cases to be heard in local hearing venues, allowing improved access to hearings through the use of existing county courts, partnerships with magistrates' courts, or hired facilities. This work will draw on the lessons learned from the use of community courts in other countries, especially in relation to security. We believe that this approach could be particularly useful in dealing with offences involving anti-social behaviour.
(Home Office, 2002b)

Making court a positive experience

On the basis of what you have just read is it possible to suggest ways of making court a positive experience, both for children and parents involved in care proceedings, and for ourselves as social work practitioners in both care and criminal proceedings?

ACTIVITY 7.3

Draw up a table with three headings:

What helps make court a positive experience for

Children/young people	Parents	Social workers

This is essentially a revision exercise: many of the points have been covered in this chapter, and if you encountered any difficulties with the activity, it would be as well to look back over what you have read. To check your answers, refer to Exercise Answers, pp148–149.

CHAPTER SUMMARY

This chapter set out a number of reasons as to why courts are important arenas of accountability for social workers, and by now you should be aware of ways in which courts should be viewed as a positive element of social work practice.

The chapter set out the key ways in which social workers may be directly involved in court, through giving evidence or writing reports in particular cases. Some guidance was offered as to how social workers should prepare themselves for the court process. The roles of key professional personnel were explained, along with an overview of procedures and processes you are likely to encounter as a social worker. These are points to bear in mind particularly when attending court for the first time.

The chapter concluded with a consideration of the needs of service users in the court system. On the basis of this you were invited to draw up guidelines that will help to make court work as positive an experience as possible for everyone involved.

One final issue you may wish to think about for the future is whether the court system as it currently operates offers the best way of dealing with youth justice and children in need of care. One key issue is whether the adversarial approach that predominates in the court system is appropriate. Hunt, Macleod and Thomas (1999) in their research on care proceedings and the operation of the Children Act 1989 concluded emphatically that the model is not well suited to the needs of care cases. As we saw in Chapter 6, there is a strong move towards making youth justice less adversarial, at least for first offenders, with the introduction of Referral Orders. The Scottish youth justice system has been based since the 1970s on Children's Hearings as distinct from Youth Courts, and this has facilitated open discussions between parents, young people and the courts about reasons for offences being committed (D. Smith, 2000). Likewise there is a move towards making Family Proceedings Court procedures more informal and less intimidating, through more flexible forms of procedures with a 'round the table' discussion that may facilitate a more open discussion of a child's needs where professionals are less preoccupied with 'winning' or 'losing' the case.

FURTHER READING

If you are asked to write a pre-sentence report or prepare a statement for court you must refer to guidelines.

For youth justice these can be found at:

National Standards for Youth Justice: **www.youth-justice-board.gov.uk/YouthJusticeBoard/** with more detailed advice at **NACRO** (2003a) Pre-Sentence Reports for Young People: A Good Practice Guide (2nd edition). London: NACRO.

For care proceedings some useful guidelines are:

Cooper, P (2006) Reporting to the Court under the Children Act: A Handbook for Practitioners. London: Stationery Office:

Wilson, J (2001) A guide to interviewing children. London: Routledge.

For general advice on the role and duties of social workers in courts see:

Seymour, C and R (2007): Courtroom Skills for Social Workers. Exeter: Learning Matters.

For advice on the role of the appropriate adult see:

NACRO (2003b) Acting As An Appropriate Adult: good practice guide. London: NACRO.

WEBSITES

Appropriate Adults: **www.appropriateadult.org.uk/**

CAFCASS: **www.cafcass.gov.uk/**

Crown Prosecution Service: **www.cps.gov.uk/**

Department of Health: **www.dh.gov.uk/en/Home**

Ministry of Justice: **www.justice.gov.uk/**

NACRO: **www.nacro.org.uk/**

Youth Justice Board: **www.yjb.gov.uk/en-gb/**

Chapter 8
Providing a quality service

Introduction

This final chapter brings together a number of different topics under the heading of providing a quality service in social work. Its primary focus is the ways in which professional standards are promoted and upheld in social work. This draws attention to the legal provisions that govern the regulation of social workers themselves, social work services, and standards of care. Included in this are the relationships between social workers and services users and social workers and their employers, and the broader issue of accountability. It concludes with an examination of the use of law in social work practice, relating this to your own future as a social work practitioner.

This chapter starts with a summary of the law relating to the regulation of the social work and social care workforce. Included in this is reference to ways in which excellence in social work is promoted, since quality assurance is not just about ensuring minimum standards but also about striving for the very best. We then outline ways in which services are regulated, the primary means by which service users are assured that a basic minimum level of service is offered, especially in terms of direct services such as residential care. The focus then moves to service users themselves and issues of accountability and confidentiality. There is then a discussion of the relationship between social workers, their employers and the public. The chapter concludes with some reflections on developments in social work law, reminding you of topics not covered in this book, with some suggestions as to what you may need to study in the future in order to complete your professional training and your degree in social work.

Professional standards and promoting sound practice

Are you safe to practise?

Are you honest, trustworthy, reliable and the kind of person in whom service users, especially children, can have confidence?

For the general public to have confidence in social workers, it is essential for them to have affirmative answers to these questions. How is this achieved?

ACTIVITY 8.1

How would you set about proving that you were a person worthy to be trusted with the well-being of the most vulnerable members of the community?

Imagine yourself in the position of a service user and ask yourself what expectations you would have of social workers — not what they will do for you, but who they are. What regulations would you expect to be in place to ensure that social workers were trustworthy?

Just spend a few moments thinking about this question. If you already know part of the answer, try to set this aside and think instead of what you would devise if you were to start with a blank sheet of paper.

Most people undertaking this exercise start with a system of registration of social workers so that people can easily check that anyone who claimed to be a social worker was officially recognised as such. You would then expect registration to involve certain obligations: minimum levels of practice competence, commitment to keep up to date with practice developments, adherence to a professional code of practice, disciplinary procedures for those who failed to meet acceptable standards of probity and competence and so on. You might also expect some consistency in standards so that a social worker trained in one country met similar requirements to those trained in another. Whilst you would not expect social workers to be clones, you would most certainly expect them to share in a body of knowledge that was common. You would also expect a reasonably consistent standard of competence in skills, and might also expect them to adhere to the same principles and values, made explicit perhaps through a code of ethics. These are expectations people rightly have of other professionals such as doctors, lawyers and nurses.

Perhaps surprisingly, this requirement has come rather late into social work. Until the passing of the Care Standards Act 2000, anyone could in effect call themselves a social worker. The prime responsibility for the regulation of the social work and social care workforce now rests with the General Social Care Council, created by that Act. This body sets the regulatory framework governing training for professional qualifications in social work and is also charged with maintaining a national register of social workers. Its specific responsibilities are:

- registration of the social care workforce;

- drawing up codes of practice relating to standards of conduct of all social care workers;

- regulation of professional training: basic qualifying courses, post-qualifying courses and advanced practice awards.

In England alongside the General Social Care Council there is an organisation called Skills for Care, formerly the Training Organisation for the Personal Social Services (TOPSS). This has a wider remit in relation to the whole social care workforce which it estimates at 1 million, about 5 per cent of the entire working population, of whom 80 per cent have no formal qualifications (see Skills for Care website at the end of this chapter). This organisation produces the occupational standards which have appeared in all chapters in this book. It is an employer-led organisation whose mission is to *improve employers' confidence in the competence of their workforce; employees' confidence in their own knowledge and skills; service users' confidence in the quality of service they are receiving.* In Wales there is one organisation, the Care Council for Wales, which carries out parallel functions of both the GSCC and Skills for Care.

The public need to be assured that there are no obvious indicators that an intending social worker might pose a risk to vulnerable people. To this end the law makes special provision.

First, the rules regarding the need to declare criminal convictions when applying for a social work post are stricter when this might involve access to vulnerable people. The Rehabilitation of Offenders Act 1974 does not apply: this Act allows people not to declare certain 'spent' convictions when they apply for a job. However, social work is exempt from this so all convictions, no matter of what kind, have to be declared.

Second, the Protection of Children Act 1999 sets out specific procedures for safeguarding children by requiring employers to check police records before employing someone, and to inform the relevant government departments if incidents come to light that cast aspersions on their safety in working with children. The Act allows the Department of Health to maintain a list of people regarded as unsuitable to work with children. The Act also enables the Criminal Records Bureau to disclose information when someone seeks a child care *position*. Child care positions are those concerned with the provision of accommodation, social services, health care services, or supervision of children, and which include regular contact with children (section 12 Protection of Children Act 1999). The employer is obliged by law to check the potential employee's criminal record and the list maintained by the Department of Health, and is forbidden to employ anyone included on the list. Employers are also under a duty to report where someone, on the grounds of harming a child, is dismissed, resigns or retires to avoid dismissal, is moved to another post within the organisation, is suspended, or where information later comes to light that would have led to any of these actions (section 2 Protection of Children Act 1999). Individuals who are registered as unsuitable have rights to appeal to the Protection of Children Act 1999 Tribunal (section 4 Protection of Children Act 1999).

In addition the Department of Health maintains a separate list of individuals who are considered unsuitable to work with vulnerable adults – the POVA (Protection of Vulnerable Adults) list (Part 7 Care Standards Act 2000). This will become the *adults' barred list* once the Safeguarding Vulnerable Groups Act 2006 is implemented, probably in 2008. The new legislation continues with separate lists of people barred from working with children (the *children's barred list*) and adults, but modifies the current system by creating a centralised vetting process, applicable to anyone who works with children or vulnerable adults in any capacity, paid or unpaid. There will be an Independent Barring Board which will make decisions about whether an individual should be included in one or both barred lists, with rights of appeal to the Care Standards Tribunal.

It is also worth noting some specific aspects of legislation that recognise the need to enhance protection for the vulnerable, for example the creation of the offence of abuse of trust in the Sexual Offences Act 2003 (sections 16–19).

Now to the more positive side: the promotion of excellence. To achieve this, the government established the Social Care Institute for Excellence as part of its Best Value strategy (Department of Health, 2000a). The purpose of the Institute is to promote quality and continuous improvement in social care through research, evidence-based knowledge primarily based on views and experience of users and together with analyses from the Commission for Social Care Inspection. It is essentially an organisation dedicated to dissemination of information, but also has a role in commissioning research, which has recently included an analysis of teaching social work law that you may find particularly interesting (Braye *et al.*, 2005).

Quality assurance of services and standards of care

CASE STUDY

The Fitzsimons family are looking for a residential home for Shelagh who is in her early nineties and finding it increasingly difficult to cope on her own. Shelagh was widowed two years ago and is still finding it strange to be alone and would welcome some company. The family want to know how they can be assured of the quality of the residential home. How do they know it will be well run? How do they know that the residents will be treated with respect? How do they know that the home will provide the special diet Shelagh needs and also respect her desire to attend the local Roman Catholic church regularly?

The quality of residential care is overseen by a central government financed body, the Commission for Social Care Inspection, a non-departmental public body, partially funded by registration fees, that was created by the Health and Social Care (Community Health and Standards) Act 2003. In Wales these functions are performed by the Care and Social Services Inspectorate Wales. These Inspectorates cover both social care and health establishments and agencies, but note that the English body no longer covers children's services. The Inspectorate will be the organisation of greatest direct interest to the Fitzsimons family since a primary objective is to regulate the quality of care and provision in individual homes and through individual organisations. It is the regulatory body charged with inspection, enforcing minimum national standards, and investigating specific complaints where these arise.

Generally speaking, both Inspectorates are responsible for registration and inspection of care services for adults in all sectors and settings, including the private and voluntary sectors. In addition, the Welsh body is responsible for care services to children, whilst in England these responsibilities have now been incorporated into the work of Ofsted, the Office for Standards in Education, Children's Services and Skills (Part 8 Education and Inspections Act 2006). Specifically Ofsted are now responsible for overall level of services for children in local authority areas, the work of CAFCASS (Children and Family Courts Advisory Service), together with inspection of childminders, day care, and adoption and fostering agencies. A separate body, the Healthcare Commission in England or the Health Care Inspectorate for Wales, is responsible for inspection of standards and enforcement in relation to health care providers, with the Mental Health Act Commission having responsibility in both countries for certain aspects of mental health care.

It is planned for some amalgamation of these various bodies to take place from 2008 onwards in order to provide a comprehensive system of inspection of health, social care and education.

What aspects of the legislation would be particularly relevant in Shelagh's case?

As with a great deal of health and social care legislation, the precise way in which the law is to be effected is governed through Regulations and nowadays also through national minimum standards. Here of greatest relevance would be the Care Homes Regulations 2001 and Department of Health guidance and standards laid down in Care Homes for Older People (Department of Health, 2003a). Briefly, the Regulations (by virtue of section 22 Care Standards Act 2000) will cover such issues as:

- the suitability of the managers, employees and premises;

- the quality of provision for welfare, management and operational procedures;

- ensuring there are sufficient staff with a minimal level of training;

- oversight of financial aspects.

National standards cover the kinds of issues more likely to be of day-to-day concern to residents and their families, such as health care, medication, privacy, meals, social activities, washing facilities, heating, furniture and fittings, and dealing with residents' money. Under these broad headings will come specific issues such as respecting Shelagh's desire to practise her religion: this is covered in Standard 12 (Department of Health, 2003a).

At a much broader level, the family might be interested in the national work of the Commission for Social Care Inspection, Ofsted and Care and Social Services Inspectorate Wales since these Inspectorates check the overall quality of services offered throughout the social care system, and sometimes evaluate local authorities themselves through a 'star rating' system. They have an important role in advising the central government and the Welsh Assembly ministers, and also in providing readily accessible information to service users and policymakers. They are also required to produce annual reports which are available on their respective websites (for details see end of chapter).

Social workers and service users

Here we are focusing on two specific issues concerning the relationship between social workers and service users in the context of responsibility for the quality of service. The first issue is accountability, especially when things appear to be going wrong; the second is confidentiality and the extent to which social workers are under an obligation to respect this.

Accountability

ACTIVITY 8.2

Imagine you are a residential social worker working in a home that offers long-term support to adults with learning disabilities in care. You become aware that some of the residents are frightened of one particular member of staff, but will not tell you what it is that is making them frightened. Your attempts to raise this with the senior management of the establishment are frustrated – you are told that you are imagining the problem and appearing frightened is a ploy to get your attention. Totally dissatisfied with this ludicrous response, you consider finding yourself another job but realise that you are under an obligation to do something.

What would you do?

The whole notion of accountability is by no means straightforward (Braye and Preston-Shoot, 2001). The ultimate question for social workers is: accountability to whom? Certainly social workers would want to consider themselves accountable to service users for the quality of services they offer. Yet social workers are clearly accountable to their employers since they pay their salaries and lay down policies and procedures which they expect employees to follow. This is as true of a voluntary organisation as it is of a local authority. A third dimension to accountability is responsibility to professional bodies and codes of ethics. In social work the British Association of Social Workers has set out guidelines of ethical practice which professional practitioners should observe, and there is a more general code of practice issued by the General Social Care Council which you are obliged to observe as a registered student social worker (see website list at end of chapter to access these codes).

In the exercise you have just tried, you as a social worker will clearly be torn several ways. First, you will want to do something for the service user who is in distress. Second, you realise that the senior managers are in effect your employers and they are the ones with the power. They are, of course, themselves accountable so you may have to consider going above them to the trustees if it is a voluntary organisation, the owners if it is a private organisation, or the members (councillors) if it is a local authority. Third, you are under a professional obligation not to walk out on service users in need. There is a strong ethical requirement for you to do something.

As far as service users are concerned, there are two ways of looking at the issue of accountability. One is simply to argue that service users are consumers and therefore if they are dissatisfied with the quality of service, they will presumably go elsewhere. This was a strong driving force behind the privatisation of much residential care for adults in the 1980s, but one objection to this is that it fails to recognise the relative powerlessness of service users. In the free market, it may be difficult for those who cannot speak for themselves and lack effective advocates. Another approach is to say that social work promotes a participative approach that sees service users as partners – hence the notion of partnership is a key principle underpinning the operation of the Children Act 1989. Again, though, it could be argued that this fails fully to recognise the power imbalance between social workers and service users and sometimes, as we saw in Chapter 4, there is an underlying question as to who is the person in most need and who exactly should be the partners.

What does the law say? First and foremost, the law draws a distinction between the needs of adults and children. In the case of children it is assumed that parents, or people acting in a parental capacity, will have the right to 'speak for' children. Therefore in the case scenario described, had the home catered for children rather than adults, there would have been a much stronger obligation on the social worker to act to prevent abuse. In the case of a local authority this would have connected to their obligations under section 47 Children Act 1989 (see Chapter 4). In the case of adults, their vulnerability is not explicitly recognised, as we saw in Chapter 5. There is a common law obligation to prevent people coming to serious harm, but this really relates to extreme circumstances – danger of accidental death or suicide, for example.

What does the law say regarding an organisation running the home that fails to take complaints of possible ill-treatment seriously? The answer to this has already been covered in this chapter: reference needs to be made to the Commission charged with implementing the Care Standards Act 2000 and the obligations under the guidance to have procedures to address possible abuse. However, you will no doubt realise that 'blowing the whistle' on what is going on in any organisation is a dangerous business. There is a very real risk of repercussions for the social worker themselves. Here the Public Interest Disclosure Act 1999 may help. The need for this legislation was recognised as a result of the Waterhouse Inquiry (Department of Health, 2000d) which acknowledged the very important role of Alison Taylor, the care worker who tried repeatedly to report the systematic sexual abuse of boys in care to the authorities (Ells and Dehn, 2001). The Act sets out a clear framework for protecting workers who raise issues of concern within their organisations, and also offers protection for wider public disclosures where initial attempts to raise issues have been thwarted.

The whole notion of professional accountability in social work is now strengthened by the introduction, in April 2005, of a professional register that attempts to put social work on the same footing as the medical and health care professions. One clear expectation is that social workers will not tolerate abuse and will report their concerns promptly and appropriately. It is not sufficient for social workers simply to say that they are 'just' employees or that it is 'more than their job's worth' to highlight malpractice. So in the case scenario you were given, the social worker should proceed up through the management structure of the organisation and keep going until the matter is investigated properly.

Confidentiality

One important feature of a quality service is the extent to which it honours the principle of confidentiality. Most people are aware of the confidentiality of their relationship with their GP, and many would expect a similar relationship with a social worker. However, we need to be careful since there are clear limitations on the extent of confidentiality. Naturally, social work is committed to the principle that information between social worker and service user can only be shared by agreement, but there are occasions when information must be shared regardless of objections. What are the exceptions to this principle that information may only be shared by agreement?

First, the principle would clearly not apply where the service user is a child and not yet able to give informed consent about disclosure of information. It is a clear principle in law that information may be disclosed if it is necessary to protect the child's health or well-being, and must be disclosed to other agencies where necessary to protect the child (HM Government, 2006). In this sense disclosure is in the interests of the service user if we accept the child as the service user – and the overriding message from review of child abuse inquiries is that we must (Department of Health, 1991a).

There may be other circumstances where there is a risk of harm to others, for example where someone has a serious mental health problem and endangers the safety of others. In one case (W *v* Edgell [1989] 1 All ER 1089) the court ordered the disclosure of a psychiatric report despite objections in these circumstances. Where social workers have a statutory duty to assess likely harm to the public, as is the case of Approved Social Workers considering compulsory admission under the Mental Health Act 1983, of necessity they are going to breach some aspects of the confidentiality principle, but nevertheless must still be careful about the extent to which they disclose information.

There have been a number of other cases involving disclosures of information in court cases, particularly in relation to child abuse. These generally have followed the line that disclosure of confidential information will be tolerated if necessary to protect the interests of children, but only in so far as it is truly necessary to reveal it (for a full discussion see Brayne and Carr, 2005, Chapter 4)

As regards the disclosure of information, two Acts of Parliament are now relevant. The Data Protection Act 1998, as implemented for social work in the Data Protection (Subject Access Modification) (Social Work) Order 2000, accords service users rights to access information about themselves. The guidelines issued by the Department of Health point out that, with a very few exceptions, people are entitled to access information about themselves, either held in conventional files or electronically, but only about themselves (Department of Health, 2000b, 5.4, 5.5). The guidelines further point out that local authorities have a general duty in common law to safeguard the confidentiality of personal information (6.2). Disclosing information without consent is permissible only where this is *reasonable in all circumstances*. Local authorities are obliged to consider requests from children and young people for access to their own files, and where they consider that the child or young person has sufficient understanding, they must accede to this request (5.8).

The other relevant Act is the Freedom of Information Act 2000, now fully implemented. This act gives a general right to information held by public authorities: central government, local authorities, the NHS, the police and schools. However, this is not to be used for obtaining information about other people, but can be used to access documents used by public authorities in carrying out any of their functions. Its purpose is to create openness to information and to enhance public accountability (for further information see the Information Commissioner's website at the end of this chapter).

Social workers, their employers and the public

To what extent are social workers accountable to the public at large and how should social workers and their employers interpret their mutual obligations?

In the case of local authority social workers, lines of accountability are fairly clear. Social workers often work in teams and therefore the person responsible for day-to-day oversight of the quality of social work will be a team manager. Above the team manager will be more senior managers, headed by a Director of Social Services or Director of Children's Services. Local authorities are obliged by law to appoint a chief officer (Local Authority Social Services Act 1970, Children Act 2004). The Director in turn is responsible to a committee, cabinet or lead member of the local authority and at this level those who hold ultimate power and responsibility will be elected members. This is important since it provides the crucial element of democratic accountability on which local government relies. We might also note that this differentiates social work, locally responsible to elected councillors, from the health service whose employees are locally responsible to non-elected NHS Trusts.

In the case of voluntary or private organisations, lines of accountability may be somewhat different. It is generally held that both kinds of organisations tend to have a 'flatter' hierarchy than local authorities. In private organisations accountability will be to an owner or company board. In voluntary organisations there may be boards, councils, trustees or management committees, almost replicating the local authority structure (Harris, 2001). Whatever the organisation, as an employer it is entitled to expect certain standards of work from its employees and may take disciplinary action where this is not the case. In cases of professional misjudgements perhaps more to be feared are the consequences of ending up in front of some kind of judicial inquiry, as has happened to social workers in the Cleveland and Climbié Inquiries (DHSS, 1988; Department of Health and Home Office, 2003). The other potential consequence is to be sued by the service user for compensation although in reality it is more likely that someone would successfully sue the employer – they are more likely to be able to pay. As we saw in the Bedfordshire case (Z and others *v* the United Kingdom [2001] 2 FLR 612) because of the consequences of implementing the Human Rights Act 1998 the courts can no longer grant local authorities immunity from legal action for persistent failure to carry out their duties.

If social workers are asked to act in some kind of court capacity, writing a report to court, advising the court or giving evidence to it, they must understand that their first duty then is to the court. They are under an obligation to give full and complete information to the court, even if this conflicts with the interests of service users or the interests of their employers. Written records may have to be made available to others despite the usual rules of confidentiality. Answers have to be given to questions (even if the social worker would prefer not to) and must be truthful, otherwise the social worker will be committing perjury. Once written evidence is submitted to court, it becomes the property of the court, and may not be disclosed for other purposes without permission from the court.

137

What are the employers' duties and obligations to their social workers? First, along with all employers they have a duty of care to their employees. In an important test case for social work (Walker *v* Northumberland County Council [1995] IRLR 35) the court awarded substantial compensation to a social worker who suffered serious psychiatric consequences as a result of work-related stress. Compensation has been awarded where social workers have demonstrated that their employer knew of the excessive degree of stress they were suffering, that there was something they could have done about it, but failed to do so.

Social work and the law

In Chapter 1 we set out a number of ways in which the law is a key component in social work practice. It was explained that the law informs social workers about what their powers, duties and responsibilities are. We have now seen that in the field of child care particularly, the law is quite extensive. It relates not just to Acts of Parliament themselves, but also to Regulations, Codes of Guidance and Circulars. In the field of adult care in particular we need to keep a sharp eye on the distinction between duties, that is the law that says what we must do, and permissive powers which set out what local authorities may do. As we saw in Chapter 5 there is not a great deal of adult care law that is actually mandatory, which contrasts quite markedly with the position in child care law covered in Chapters 3 and 4. It is also in this field that the law has intervened most, setting out lines of accountability, and in Chapter 7 we focused on the courts which in the UK, perhaps more than in any other country, play a key role in setting out the boundaries between the state, parents and child. Social workers in Britain maintain a high level of accountability to the courts, since they offer an ultimate avenue of appeal when service users feel that they have been dealt with unfairly or unjustly. In areas such as mental health, the law helps to demarcate that fine line between the individual's right to self-determination and the duty of social workers to intervene to protect others (Chapter 5, protecting vulnerable adults). In child protection cases the courts endorse or reject decisions made by social work agencies. Summarising all of this we can see that in all areas, the courts are invaluable in offering a neutral, independent and authoritative venue where social work decisions can be tested and social workers publicly held to account. This may not be terribly comfortable at the time, but it is an important safeguard in any system where social workers still work primarily in the state sector and therefore have considerable power.

Inevitably the law has greatest impact on local authority social workers, but social workers in all spheres, employed by a whole variety of different kinds of organisations, need to know the basics of how the law regulates social work. By now you should be well aware of how the law serves to set the boundaries within which social work operates. It is hoped that you can also now see how the law can be used positively in order to promote people's rights, to protect them from infringements of their basic freedoms and to further their interests. The book was deliberately entitled 'Using the law in social work' and it is hoped that by this point you begin to see how law can be used in order to empower social work service users and how it is a positive tool in social work practice.

So what's next?

Review and the future: what next?

The law that has been covered here should be more than adequate for the attainment of benchmarks and National Occupational Standards at Level one of the BA or start of the MA. At higher levels you may require more specialist information about the law and how it operates in social work so in this section there is a brief overview of areas of law that we have not examined in detail, followed by an exposition of potential future changes which will incorporate some suggestions for further study.

To remind you, at the outset it was declared that the book would not examine social security law although this will be an important area if you intend to work as a social worker in some kind of advocacy role. Allied with this is the law relating to asylum seekers and refugees. This is a specialist area in social work of particular importance in relation to unaccompanied children and young people, but unfortunately beyond the scope of this book. Key legislation here is the Immigration and Asylum Act 1999, the Nationality, Immigration and Asylum Act 2002, the Asylum and Immigration (Treatment of Claimants, etc.) Act 2004 and the Immigration, Asylum and Nationality Act 2006 (for further information see Brammer, 2007, Chapter 20; Brayne and Carr, 2005, Chapter 21). We have also not covered housing law, either in terms of homelessness, tenancy protection or issues that arise when people wish to live together as a unit (the most relevant legislation in these areas being the Homelessness Act 2002, the Housing Act 2004 and the Civil Partnership Act 2004). If you are engaged in advocacy or advice work concerning the break-up of relationships, you may wish to know more about the law regarding domestic violence than is contained in this book; for example, we have not addressed the detailed procedures under the Family Law Act 1996 as amended and extended by the Domestic Violence, Crime and Victims Act 2004 for obtaining occupation orders and non-molestation orders or the implications of non-compliance with injunctions.

In Chapter 5 there was brief reference to the Mental Health Act 1983 in the context of protecting vulnerable adults, but mental health legislation has a number of other facets. Social workers with post-qualifying experience sometimes opt to become Approved Social Workers, who have the power and authority to arrange compulsory admissions under the Mental Health Act 1983. Proposed legislation may change this in future, but suffice it to say that it requires much more detailed knowledge and practice experience than would be expected at this stage, including attendance at a post-qualifying Care Council approved training course. Also under mental health law, we have not examined guardianship, a form of supervision of people with *mental disorders*, or the law relating to tribunals and their expectations of social workers, although this was mentioned in passing. If you work with vulnerable adults, you may want to find out more about the Mental Capacity Act 2005 regarding capacity to consent and managing one's own affairs.

Whilst Chapter 6 covered youth justice, this book has made no attempt to cover adult criminal law as this is outside the area of responsibility of social workers in England and Wales. However if you intend to practise in Scotland or Northern Ireland, the situation is quite different. Scottish social workers in particular do need to know about the provisions of the adult criminal justice system. Although there was some reference to the police powers in criminal investigations in Chapter 6, with reference to the role of social workers acting as *appropriate adults*, it was not really feasible to cover the rules governing police procedures which are mainly to be found in the Police and Criminal Evidence Act 1984, associated Codes of Practice, and amendments to be introduced by the Police and Justice Act 2006.

Two other areas have not been covered. Access to financial support for service users involved in court cases, either as litigants or as victims, has not featured in this book. For this reference needs to be made to legal aid provision (for which the Legal Services Commission is responsible) and to the criminal injury compensation scheme (for which the Criminal Injury Compensation Authority is responsible). Nor has there been detailed consideration of anti-discrimination legislation for reasons that were explained in Chapter 1 although there have been several references to the Race Relations (Amendment) Act 2000 and its requirement that local authorities and other public bodies take a proactive stance in relation to racial and ethnic discrimination, to which should now be added a proactive stance towards disability discrimination (Disability Discrimination Act 2005).

Now to possible future developments.

Chapter 2 looked at the increasing importance of the European Convention on Human Rights in UK law. There will undoubtedly be further cases addressing the relationship between the state and the individual. Currently concern centres on anti-terrorism laws, restrictions on asylum seekers, political involvement in determining the sentences for people convicted of serious offences and the interpretation of people's entitlement to privacy.

In Chapters 3 and 4, we looked at the extensive field of childcare law where there are a number of issues. The Children Act 2004 is key here. The Act is being implemented in stages but it is already having a significant impact on the organisation of social services, with a clear demarcation emerging between adults' services and children's services. Likewise the Adoption and Children Act 2002 is beginning to have a major impact on practice, although its significance in relation to adoption could not be fully explored here. However, if you intend to practise in this area you will need to learn more about this legislation and its implications for practice. Whilst there are no plans declared so far for changing the basic provisions of the Children Act 1989, the Childcare Act 2006 marks a significant step towards integrated services for younger children, along with support for working parents, and it will be interesting to chart its progress once it begins to be implemented.

The field of adult care law has been crying out for a long time for legal reform, and as explained in Chapter 5, there is a pressing need for codification of the law regarding service provision and informed consent. This has now been partly remedied with the implementation of the Mental Capacity Act 2005, which sets out a single clear test for determining whether someone *lacks capacity*. Fairly soon there may well be changes in mental health legislation so as to broaden its scope and potentially bring people with personality disorders within the remit of compulsory control and extend compulsory powers to cover people who are deemed to need supervision rather than treatment. Despite a barrage of criticism, the government has declared that it may press on regardless with its proposals to control a minority of people perceived to be dangerous. This is particularly regrettable as there appear to be no plans to try to create a charter of rights of entitlement to services for people with mental health problems, and you will undoubtedly have noticed the strong contrast between the lack of real substantive rights for vulnerable adults compared to the entitlement to services of children in need.

The field of youth justice (Chapter 6) is always politically sensitive and again there will probably be some changes and development here. Currently there is concern about the need to prevent crime in the pre-teen years, with an attempt to introduce preventative youth justice measures. The anti-social behaviour orders in the Crime and Disorder Act 1998 were not widely used when first introduced, but recently courts have being encouraged to use them more frequently and more widely, aided by the passing of the Anti-Social Behaviour Act 2003. Again there is virulent opposition to this in some quarters. You may recall that these orders are not made as a result of proven criminal acts but are civil measures taken where the courts are persuaded on the balance of probabilities that there is a likelihood of committing offences. There may even be some doubt as to whether anti-social behaviour orders conform to the European Convention on Human Rights.

Looking at court work, the subject of Chapter 7, major recent developments have related to the organisation and administration of the courts themselves following implementation of the Courts Act 2003. This provided for a unified national courts administration service, Her Majesty's Courts Service established in April 2005, charged with delivering improved services to the community, victims, witnesses and all other users of the courts.

In this chapter we noted developments in relation to the Inspectorates, who appear to be broadening their scope and now comment both on social care policy implementation and quality of standards in individual establishments and organisations. We also noted other measures designed to protect service users and promote professional standards, including, finally, the area that has most direct immediate impact on you – the Care Standards Act 2000. Its professional registration requirements, both for social work practitioners and student social workers, are now fully implemented. You, as a student social worker, are required to abide by the professional codes of practice for social work so you need to know what these are. You also need to be registered with the General Social Care Council (for England) or the Care Council for Wales. If you are not already registered, please put down this book now and go on to the relevant Council's website immediately.

FURTHER READING

For national minimum standards in care homes see:

Department of Health (2003a) Care Homes for Older People (3rd edition). London: Stationery Office.

For further discussion of the role of law in social work see:

Cull, L and Roche, J (2001) The Law and Social Work. Basingstoke: Palgrave.

WEBSITES

BASW for Code of Ethics: **www.basw.co.uk/**

Care Council for Wales: **www.ccwales.org.uk/**

Commission for Social Care Inspection: **www.csci.org.uk/**

Care and Social Services Inspectorate Wales: **www.csiw.wales.gov.uk/index.asp**

Criminal Injuries Compensation Authority: **www.cica.gov.uk/**

Department of Health – quality strategy for social care: **www.dh.gov.uk/en/Publicationsandstatis tics/Publications/PublicationsPolicyAndGuidance/DH_4007144**; protection of vulnerable adults: **www.dh.gov.uk/assetRoot/04/09/03/19/04090319.pdf**

General Social Care Council (GSCC): **www.gscc.org.uk**; codes of practice for social care workers and employers: **www.gscc.org.uk/Good+practice+and+conduct/Get+copies+of+our+codes/**

Information Commissioner: **www.informationcommissioner.gov.uk/eventual.aspx?id=33**

Legal Services Commission: **www.legalservices.gov.uk/**

Office for Standards in Education (Ofsted): **www.ofsted.gov.uk/**

Social Care Institute for Excellence (SCIE): **www.scie.org.uk/**

Skills for Care (formerly Training Organisation for the Personal Social Services; TOPSS): **www.topssengland.net/**

Exercise answers

Chapter 1
Activity 1.3

	Statute law	Common law
Criminal law	Crime and Disorder Act 1998 Theft Act 1968 Sexual Offences Act 2003	Once found not guilty of an offence by the court a defendant cannot usually be retried People who are accused of crimes are assumed innocent until found guilty Actively assisting someone to commit suicide is murder
Civil law	Failing to pay a TV licence fee Chronically Sick and Disabled Persons Act 1970 National Health Service and Community Care Act 1990 All employees must be provided with a contract of employment Family Law Act 1996 Care Home Regulations 2001	Failing to pay rent An employer's duty of care to employees Spending money on a service which a local authority does not have statutory authority to provide means it is acting *ultra vires*

Chapter 2
Activity 2.2

European Convention on Human Rights

Article 1	The convention applies to everyone.
Article 2	Right to life. Some exemptions: execution as court sentence use of force in defence of someone subject to unlawful violence lawful arrest or prevention of escape from custody to quell a riot or insurrection

Article 3	No one shall be subjected to torture or to inhuman or degrading treatment or punishment.
Article 4	No slavery or forced labour. Limited exemptions for prisoners, military service, time of war.
Article 5	Right to *liberty and security of person*. Exceptions: (a) detention following conviction by court; (b) arrest and detention for non-compliance with law; (c) arrest or detention in order to bring before court on suspicion of committing offence; (d) detention of young people in relation to education; (e) *the lawful detention of persons for the prevention of the spreading of infectious diseases, of persons of unsound mind, alcoholics or drug addicts, or vagrants;* (f) arrest in relation to deportation or extradition. There are additional provisions in relation to arrest. Some of these are referred to later in chapter. Note especially (e) above.
Article 6	Right to trial. Innocent until proven guilty. List of minimum rights set out in relation to people charged with criminal offences.
Article 7	No retrospective convictions, i.e. cannot be prosecuted for an action that was lawful at the time it was committed.
Article 8	*Everyone has the right to respect for his private and family life, his home and his correspondence.* *There shall be no interference by public authority with the exercise of this right except such as is an accordance with the law and is necessary in a democratic society in the interests of national security, public safety or the economic well-being of the country, for the prevention of disorder or crime, for the protection of health or morals, or for the protection of the rights and freedoms of others.*
Article 9	Right to *freedom of thought, conscience and religion*. This includes right to change religions and the freedom to *manifest* religion or belief in worship, teaching, practice and observance. Exceptions must be in the interests of public safety or protection of public order, health or morals or protection of the rights and freedoms of others.
Article 10	Rights of freedom of expression. Several exemptions acknowledging that this carries duties and responsibilities: underlying criterion here is *necessary in a democratic society*.
Article 11	Rights of assembly and association. Again exemptions as are necessary in a democratic society.
Article 12	Right to marry and *found a family*.
Article 13	Rights to an effective remedy for violation of Convention.
Article 14	No discrimination in applying Convention rights.

N.B. Above table is a summary with partial quotations. For complete European Convention on Human Rights see: **www.echr.coe.int/Convention/webConvenENG.pdf**

Potential relevance of Convention to social work and service users

Of the Articles of the Convention, those which appear to be particularly relevant to social work are (in Convention order, not necessarily potential order of importance):

Article 2	euthanasia, abortion (although European court has tried to steer clear of this one), medical decision-making and capacity to make informed medical choices
Article 3	failure to protect from harm (Bedfordshire case – see below), physical punishment of children, standards of care in homes, treatment in psychiatric hospitals and prisons
Article 5	detention of people with mental disorder capacity to consent to hospital admission asylum seekers political interference in court sentences
Article 6	arrest rights right to fair trial discharge from prison discharge from secure hospitals
Article 8	routine checking of correspondence: prisons, hospitals surveillance equipment rights of patients and service users to nominate nearest relative
Article 10	confidentiality press coverage of particular cases
Article 12	position of transsexuals changing birth data
Article 13	denying children access to remedies (Bedfordshire case)

Chapter 3

Activity 3.3

The government schemes introduced since 1997 are (in brief):

Quality Protects

Quality Protects is a policy initiative launched in 1998 which aims at the effective protection, quality care and improved life chances for children (Department of Health, 1998a, 1998b, 2000a). It does this through establishing specific objectives for children's services both nationally and locally, and through promoting partnership between government agencies and the voluntary sector.

Surestart

The Surestart programme brings together early education, health and family support in order to address disadvantage and social exclusion. It promotes universal early education and improved child care, through for example children's centres and specific local programmes. Its principles are very similar to those undergirding the Children Act 1989: working in partnership with parents, services offered according to need, flexibility, responsiveness to what parents want, together with an emphasis on community links and simpler funding mechanisms.

Children's Fund

The Children's Fund focuses on 5–13-year-olds, social exclusion and poverty. It aims to promote multi-agency working in identifying children where there are early signs of difficulties, providing family support to create long-term improvement, operating on the principle of involving children, young people and parents in planning services. The emphasis is very much on flexible preventative services that meet local communities' needs.

Children's National Service Framework

The Children's National Service Framework, a programme established in 2001, sets out national standards for the National Health Service and social services for children. These are intended to break down professional boundaries and promote partnership, allowing easier access to services and enabling statutory agencies to focus on needs.

Children's Taskforce

The aim of the Children's Taskforce is to improve children's health through needs-led, integrated, evidence-based services (see website list). It is focused on the NHS National Plan but also is responsible for implementing the Children's National Service Framework.

You will find further information on the website listed at the end of Chapter 3.

Chapter 4
Activity 4.2

In the first scenario, it is very likely that you concluded that children of this age are terrified at being left alone even for a short time, although clearly you would want to know more about the circumstances. However the question also arises what kind of abuse would this be potentially? No direct physical harm is caused, so you might conclude that this is neglect.

Scenario 2 is more problematic since many would consider the parents' expectations quite reasonable, and therefore not abusive. However, if this were to be considered abuse, what kind of abuse would it be? It is not neglect, but it could be argued that excessive demands on children impede their intellectual or emotional development (although unlikely in this case).

Most people would conclude that scenario 3 is highly abusive since, although not directly physically harmful, it is quite terrifying to children to be locked in a confined space even for a short time.

Scenario 4 appears to be a clear-cut case of physical abuse but one might want to know how the injuries were caused – or perhaps you wouldn't: does it matter if it's a dog bite or the consequences of being bitten by another child?

Scenario 5 raises the issue of sexual abuse but also the possibility of the need to take into account both children as victims and abusers.

The final scenario would now be considered an obvious case of physical abuse, although relatively common standard child care practice until fairly recently. Indeed beating children with an implement now appears to be a direct contravention of the European Convention on Human Rights (see cases summarised in Chapter 2).

Chapter 5

Activity 5.3

There is no specific law that promotes empowerment as such, but there are various pieces of legislation that promote rights to advocacy and representation and choice, together with anti-discrimination legislation. You could have referred to some of the following.

Carers and Disabled Children Act 2000 and/or Carers (Recognition and Services) Act 1995	carers' rights
Chronically Sick and Disabled Persons Act 1970; National Health Service and Community Care Act 1990	local authority duty to provide information on services
Community Care (Direct Payments) Act 1996	right to choose and pay own service provider
Disabled Persons (Services, Consultation and Representation) Act 1986	advocacy rights for people with disabilities
Disability Discrimination Act 1995; Disability Rights Commission Act 1999	anti-discriminatory law
Human Rights Act 1998	various rights from European Convention on Human Rights incorporated into UK law
Mental Health Act 1983	appeal rights
Race Relations Act 1976; Race Relations Amendment Act 2000	anti-discriminatory law, requirements to be pro-active in promoting good race relations

In terms of service provision, you may have referred to the regulatory duties of inspection (these are covered in detail in Chapter 8). Relevant here would be the Care Standards Act 2000. Also relevant would be:

- regulations: for example, regarding choice of accommodation;

- local authority circulars (LACs): for example, regarding quality assurance and best value;

- Codes of Practice: regarding sensitive practice in matters such as mental health;

- National Service Frameworks: for older people, mental health and White Paper on Learning Disabilities all set out ways of achieving good practice but these do not themselves have the full force of law. They set standards by which central government makes judgements about the quality of services so may carry financial rather than legal weight.

For full discussion of the status and standing of Regulations, Circulars and Codes of Practice see Chapter 1.

Chapter 6
Activity 6.2

Sources of possible avenues for research:

- books, not just textbooks but also biographical and autobiographical accounts;

- articles in refereed journals (possibly accessed through databases);

- articles in professional journals;

- articles in newspapers – do be careful here, given the media tendency to sensationalise;

- service users themselves, obviously, although do pay close attention to issues such of sensitivity and confidentiality;

- practitioners in the youth justice field, although be careful about how much time you take up;

- information from research bodies such as the Joseph Rowntree Trust or RPS Rayner (these are only examples, there are plenty of others);

- information from groups representing the interests of users such as victim support groups, either published information or personal visits – but again do be careful how much time you take up if you visit them;

- internet sources: although again pay great attention to the reliability and authenticity of the websites you use.

Chapter 7
Activity 7.3

Answers to Activity 7.3 ought to have included at least the following:

The key issues for children are:

- keeping them aware of what is happening;

- presenting information in a way that they can understand;

- clarifying their wishes and feelings;

- ensuring that wishes and feelings are properly conveyed to the court.

The key issues for parents are:

- understanding what is happening to them;
- obtaining sound legal advice and assistance;
- openness and transparency;
- social workers being honest about issues.

The key issues for social workers are:

- being straight with people about issues involved;
- continuing to work in partnership with parents;
- proper preparation of cases for court;
- testing out evidence, being clear about the difference between facts, interpretation of facts, and opinion;
- maintaining objectivity and impartiality.

References

Adams, R (2002) Social policy for social work. Basingstoke: Palgrave.

Alcock, P, Erskine, A and May, M [eds] (2003) The student's companion to social policy (2nd edition). Oxford: Blackwell.

Aldgate, J (2001) The Children Act now: messages from research: studies in evaluating the Children Act 1989. London: Stationery Office.

Ariès, P (1979) Centuries of childhood. Harmondsworth: Penguin.

Association of Directors of Social Services (ADSS) (2005) Safeguarding adults: a national framework of standards for good practice and outcomes in adult protection work. London: ADSS.

Baldock, J and Ungerson, C (1994) Becoming consumers of community care: households within the mixed economy of welfare. Abingdon: Policy Press.

Ball, C and McDonald, A (2002) Law for social workers (4th edition). London: Ashgate.

Bhabra, S, Ghate, D and Brazier, L (2002) Raising the educational attainment of children in care. London: Policy Research Bureau.

Bostock, L, Bairstow, S, Fish, S, and Macleod, F (2005) Managing risk and minimizing mistakes in services to children and families. Bristol: Policy Press for SCIE (Social Care Institute for Excellence).

Brammer, A (2007) Social work law (2nd edition). London: Pearson.

Braye, S (2000) Disabled children and social care: law and practice in Cooper, J. (ed.) Law, rights and disability. London: Jessica Kingsley.

Braye, S and Preston-Shoot, M (2001) Social work practice and accountability in Cull, L and Roche, J (2001) The law and social work. Basingstoke: Palgrave.

Braye, S and Preston-Shoot, M, with Cull, L-A, Johns, R and Roche, J (2005) Teaching, learning and assessment of law in social work education. London: Social Care Institute for Excellence/Policy Press.

Brayne, H and Broadbent, G (2002) Legal materials for social workers. Oxford: Oxford University Press.

Brayne, H and Carr, H (2005) Law for social workers (9th edition). Oxford: Oxford University Press.

Brown, H and Smith, H (eds) (1992) Normalisation: a reader for the nineties. London: Tavistock/Routledge.

Clarke, J (1993) A crisis in care: challenges to social work. London: Sage.

Clements, L (1996) Community care and the law. London: Legal Action Group.

Cooper, P (2006) Reporting to the Court under the Children Act: a handbook for practitioners. London: Stationery Office.

Department of Health (2004b) National Service Framework for children, young people and maternity services. London: Stationery Office.

Department of Health (2005) Independence, well-being and choice: our vision for the future of social care for adults in England. London: Stationery Office.

Department of Health (2006a) Mental Health Bill 2006. Norwich: Stationery Office.

Department of Health (2006b) Our health, our care, our say: a new direction for community services. Norwich: Stationery Office.

Department of Health and Home Office (2006e) No secrets: guidance on developing and implementing multi-agency policies and procedures to protect vulnerable adults from abuse. London: Stationery Office.

Department of Health and Home Office (2003) The Victoria Climbié inquiry: report of an inquiry by Lord Laming. London: Stationery Office.

DHSS (Department of Health and Social Security) (1974) Report of the committee of inquiry into the care and supervision provided in relation to Maria Colwell. London: HMSO.

DHSS (Department of Health and Social Security) (1988) The report of the inquiry into child abuse in Cleveland 1987 (Butler-Sloss inquiry). London: HMSO.

Dugmore, P, Pickford, J and Angus, S (2006) Youth justice and social work. Exeter: Learning Matters.

Eastman, M (1994) Old age abuse: a new perspective. London: Chapman Hall.

Ells, P and Dehn, G (2001) Whistleblowing: public concern at work in Cull L. and Roche J. (2001) The law and social work. Basingstoke: Palgrave.

Fennell, P (1999) The third way in mental health policy: negative rights, positive rights and the convention. Journal of Law and Society 26, 103–127.

Fox-Harding, L (1997) Perspectives in child care policy (2nd revised edition). London: Longman.

Freeman, P and Hunt, J (1998) Parental perspectives on care proceedings. London: HMSO.

Goldson, B (2002) Vulnerable inside: children in secure and penal settings. London: Children's Society.

Goldson, B and Muncie, J (2006) Youth crime and justice. London: Sage.

Griffiths, R (1988) Community care: agenda for action. London: HMSO.

Harris, M (2001) Boards: just subsidiaries of the state? in Harris, M and Rochester, C Voluntary organisations and social policy in Britain. Basingstoke: Palgrave.

HM Government (2006) Working together to safeguard children. Norwich: Stationery Office.

Home Office (1998) Speaking up for justice: report of the interdepartmental working group. London: Stationery Office.

Home Office (2001) Youth justice: the statutory principal aim of preventing offending by children and young people. London: Home Office.

Home Office (2002a) Achieving the best evidence in criminal proceedings: guidance for vulnerable or intimidated witnesses including children. London: Stationery Office.

Corker, M and Davis, JM (2000) Disabled children (still) invisible under the law in Cooper, J. (e Law, rights and disability. London: Jessica Kingsley.

Cowen, H (1999) Community care, ideology and social policy. Hemel Hempstead: Prentice Hall.

Cull, L and Roche, J (2001) The law and social work. Basingstoke: Palgrave.

Dalrymple, J and Burke, B (1995) Anti-oppressive practice: social care and the law. Buckingh Open University Press.

Department for Education and Skills (2004) Every child matters: change for children. Lor Stationery Office.

Department for Education and Skills (2005) Statutory guidance on the duty on local authori promote the educational achievement of looked after children under section 52 of the Childi 2004. Nottingham: DfES publications.

Department for Education and Skills (2006a) Care matters: transforming the lives of child young people in care. Norwich: Stationery Office.

Department for Education and Skills (2006b) The Children Act 1989 report 2004 ar Nottingham: DfES publications.

Department of Constitutional Affairs (2007) Mental Capacity Act 2005 code of practice Stationery Office.

Department of Health (1989) An introduction to the Children Act. London: HMSO.

Department of Health (1991a) Child abuse: a study of inquiry reports 1981–1989. Londor

Department of Health (1991b) Children Act 1989 guidance and regulations. London: HM

Department of Health (1999) National service framework for mental health modern st service models. London: Department of Health.

Department of Health (2000a) A quality strategy for social care. London: Stationery Offi

Department of Health (2000b) Data Protection Act 1998 guidance to social serv Stationery Office.

Department of Health (2000c) Framework for the assessment of children in need an London: Stationery Office.

Department of Health (2000d) Lost in care – Report of the tribunal of inquiry into the a in care in the former county council areas of Gwynedd and Clwyd since 1974. London: Sta

Department of Health (2001a) National service framework for older people. London: Dep

Department of Health (2001b) Valuing people: a new strategy for learning disal century. London: Stationery Office.

Department of Health (2003a) Care homes for older people. London: Stationery Of

Department of Health (2003b) Fair Access to Care Services LAC 2002(13). London: Dej

Department of Health (2004a) Mental Health Bill 2004. London: Stationery Office

Home Office (2002b) Justice for all. London: HMSO.

Home Office (2003) Youth justice next steps. London: HMSO.

Hunt, J, Macleod, A and Thomas, C (1999) The last resort: child protection, the courts and the 1989 Children Act. London: HMSO.

Johns, R and Sedgwick, A (1998) Law for social work practice: working with vulnerable adults. Basingstoke: Macmillan.

Johns, R (2005) Of unsound mind? Mental health social work and the European Convention on Human Rights. *Practice* 16(4) 247–259.

Jones, R (2006) Mental Health Act manual (10th edition). London: Sweet and Maxwell.

Lavalette, M and Pratt, A (2005) Social policy: a conceptual and theoretical introduction (2nd edition). London: Sage.

Law Commission (1993) Mentally incapacitated adults and decision-making: a new jurisdiction. London: HMSO.

Levy, A and Kahan, B (1991) The pindown experience and the protection of children – report of the Staffordshire Child Care Inquiry 1990. Stafford: Staffordshire County Council.

NACRO (2003a) Pre-sentence reports for young people: a good practice guide (2nd edition). London: NACRO.

NACRO (2003b) Acting as an appropriate adult: good practice guide. London: NACRO.

National Assembly for Wales (2005) Raising the standard: the revised adult mental health National Service Framework and an action plan for Wales. Cardiff: Welsh Assembly Government.

Packman, J (1975) The child's generation. Oxford: Blackwell.

Parker, J and Bradley, G (2007) Social work practice: assessment, planning, intervention and review (2nd edition). Exeter: Learning Matters.

Parton, N (1985) The politics of child abuse. Basingstoke: Macmillan.

Prior, PM (2001) Protective Europe: does it exist for people with mental disorders? Journal of European Social Policy 11(1), 25–38.

Pritchard, J (ed) (2001) Good practice with vulnerable adults. London: Jessica Kingsley.

Quality Assurance Agency for Higher Education (QAA) (2000) Social policy and administration and social work subject benchmark statements. London: QAA.

Rai-Atkins, A, Ali-Jama, A, Wright, N, Scott, V, Coy, J, Craig, G and Katbamna, S (2002) Best practice in mental health: advocacy for African, Caribbean and South Asian communities. Abingdon: Policy Press.

Raynes, N, Temple, B, Glenister, C and Coulthard, L (2001) Quality at home for older people: involving service users in defining home care specifications. Abingdon: Policy Press.

Ruegger, M (2001) Hearing the voice of the child. Lyme Regis: Russell House.

Seebohm (1968) Report of the Committee on Local Authority and Allied Personal Social Services. London: HMSO.

Seymour, C and R (2007): Courtroom skills for social workers. Exeter: Learning Matters.

Sharkey, P (2006) The essentials of community care: a guide for practitioners (2nd edition). Basingstoke: Macmillan.

Smith, D (2000) Learning from the Scottish juvenile justice system. Probation Journal 47(1), 13–17.

Smith, F (2000) Looking after children: good parenting, good outcomes. London: Children Act Enterprises.

Social Exclusion Unit (2003) A better education for children in care. London: Stationery Office.

Stephenson, M, Giller, H and Brown, S (2007) Effective practice in youth justice. Cullompton: Willan.

Sutherland (1999) With respect to old age: long term care – rights and responsibilities: a report by The Royal Commission on Long Term Care. London: Stationery Office.

Thoburn, J, Lewis, A and Shemmings, D (1995) Paternalism or partnership: family involvement in the child protection process. London: HMSO.

Thompson, N (2001) Anti-discriminatory practice (3rd edition). Basingstoke: Palgrave.

Tosey, P (2000) Making sense of interventions, in Wheal, A (ed) Working with parents: learning from other people's experience. Lyme Regis: Russell House.

Vernon, A (2002) User-defined outcomes of community care for Asian disabled people. Abingdon: Policy Press.

Vernon, S (2005) Social work and the law (3rd edition). London: Butterworths.

Welsh Assembly (2003) Health, social care and well-being strategies: policy guidance. Cardiff: Welsh Assembly Government.

Welsh Assembly (2005) Raising the standard: the revised adult mental health National Service Framework and an action plan for Wales. Cardiff: Welsh Assembly Government.

White, R, Carr, P and Lowe, N (2002) The Children Act in practice (3rd edition). London: Butterworths.

Williams, J (2002) Public law protection of vulnerable adults: the debate continues, so does the abuse. Journal of Social Work 2(3), 293–316.

Wilson, J (2001) A guide to interviewing children. London: Routledge.

Wright, F (1998) The effect on carers of a frail older person's admission to a care home. London: Age Concern.

Youth Justice Board (2004) National standards for youth justice. London: Youth Justice Board.

Youth Justice Board for England and Wales (2005) National evaluation of the bail supervision and support schemes. London: Youth Justice Board for England and Wales.

Index